SPIRITUAL WARFARE
&
THE ART OF DECEPTION

SPIRITUAL WARFARE

THE ART OF DECEPTION

The Hijacking of Spirituality

ARI KOPEL

ROUND TABLE PUBLISHERS

For information about this title or to order other books and/or electronic media, contact the publisher:

Round Table Publisher, Inc.

P.O. Box 17104

Nashville, TN 37217

RoundTablePublishers.com

info@roundtablepublishers.com

Library of Congress Control Number:

ISBN: 978-0-9861769-0-6

Printed in the United States of America

Cover and Interior design: Debbie O'Byrne

Publisher's Cataloging-In-Publication Data

(Prepared by The Donohue Group, Inc.)

Kopel, Ari.

Spiritual warfare & the art of deception: the hijacking of spirituality / by Ari Kopel.

pages: illustrations, charts ; cm

Includes index.

ISBN: 978-0-9861769-0-6

1. New Age movement--Controversial literature. 2. Spirituality. 3. Discernment of spirits. 4. Occultism. I. Title. II. Title: Spiritual warfare and the art of deception

BP605.N48 K67 2015

299/.93

To my soul mate, for making this possible and for being my teacher.

To my parents, for providing the fertile environment.

To my children, for letting me experience such profound love.

To my grandchildren, for giving me the reason to write this book.

CONTENTS

PREFACE

"The battle, sir, is not to the strong alone; it is to the vigilant, the active, the brave."

—Patrick Henry

I would consider myself an overachiever and successful at whatever I set my mind to do. When I've had laser-sharp focus on achieving a goal, I have attained that goal and more. The ability to bring into my reality whatever I wanted was part of my "wiring" and was kept active by my profound connection to a "higher" spiritual power. The close relationship I had with God-Creator and my ability to manifest what I wanted was not even something I had to think consciously about; I was just designed this way. I would think an affirmative thought about something I wanted, this thought would guide my actions, and shortly after, the thing I thought about would manifest. I became aware of this "gift" very early in my life – at age four.

After spending a good portion of my life living and acting "in the zone" or being "in the flow" of God/Prime Creator, something happened that stopped all the "magic" – if we can call it that – from happening. I couldn't figure out why I wasn't thriving anymore, why

I was feeling ill, why I was having so many interpersonal conflicts, why nothing I was doing seemed to work or give me a positive outcome. I was stuck, and I didn't know how I got there.

When I had immersed myself in the world of business, I was able to create financial wealth practically out of thin air. I used the principles of manifestation that I was familiar with that never failed me. But being in the world of commerce and having to figure out ways to earn money allowed me to observe firsthand what the term "dog-eat-dog" means. People can be ruthless when it comes to protecting their dollar or the potential of acquiring that dollar. They do things they would not normally do, even if it conflicts with their moral foundation. This aggression depicts survival of the fittest in the "Matrix" or "Rat-Race"; it is a world that not many know how to navigate and often find themselves receiving mortal wounds. Despite this, I did quite well, but after many years, I was tired of swimming in the shark-infested-waters and hungering to be with those who were noble, kind, and spiritually connected to God. With renewed purpose and passion, I dove deeper into a "morphed version" of Spirituality, with no idea that I was entering equally dangerous waters.

Soon I began to notice many inconsistencies in the information that was being freely disseminated. In fact, much of it went against what I "Knew", as I had kept my memories of a Realm from which I had originated. But because I wanted so desperately to have kinship and camaraderie with others who were seeking a new way of conduct, a new way of living – in short, a new Earth – I went along with it. It was certainly better than the money-hungry world of business. I wanted to escape the rat race and live on a farm, have chickens and grow my produce. I wanted to be self-sustainable and self-reliant. I wanted to be in unity with The All That Is, and in my search I found many commonalities with the goals of the so-called "spiritual community".

Still, those inconsistencies and falsities kept coming up, and they didn't sit well with me. On top of that, after doing my meditations, saging (filling the home with sage smoke to take away evil spirits), saying countless affirmations and what-have-you, my life was a mess. And I wondered a lot about that. My finances were tanking, and I wasn't contributing to the household because I couldn't get myself to work in "the Matrix" any longer. Something in me – that spark of joy and my manifestation capabilities – had been quashed. Now a bit jaded, I had to live in mediocrity and was barely "making it". In fact, I was counting my pennies – as most in the "spiritual community" were – except the teachers, leaders, and gurus. They lived fairly well. They lived fairly well because they were teaching others like me the secrets of the universe, the keys we needed for our Ascension or Rapture or graduation to the next level in our spiritual experience. They were okay because they charged a pretty penny for their pearls of wisdom and enlightenment. There was something not right here, and I didn't understand what had happened that unplugged me or disconnected me from my ability to manifest and become empowered.

After much introspection and objective observation, I came to a couple of conclusions, conclusions that I knew were spot on. At the same time, I found myself resisting these findings. Without realizing it, I had inadvertently joined and fallen into the trap of the New Age Movement, which included the plethora of philosophies, ideologies and concepts that, again, were in direct contradiction to what I knew from direct experience with the Illumined Realms or Kingdom of God. And as soon as I was fully immersed in it, my life changed for the worse. I went from manifesting, creating, achieving abundance and joy to lack, hardship, decline, stagnation and loneliness. "How was this possible," I would ask myself? I know how to do this; I know how to create out of nothingness, out of the ether. I could manifest money and live in abundance – yet, I was slowly and steadily withering like a flower that isn't watered regularly. I didn't know why this was happening – until I started observing a pattern, and this pattern led me to see the bigger picture and a very, very ugly truth.

I noticed that my new friends, who were also participating in this New Age "Spiritual" Movement, were all suffering as well. I didn't know one – not one – person in this movement that was thriving, who had their "stuff" together. As a matter of fact, most suffered from health issues, financial issues, relationship problems, drama and chaos. Many of them suffered from depression; were bipolar; were victims of sexual, physical, emotional and/or verbal abuse; were in or had been in bad marriages; were bullied; had self-esteem issues; identity issues, or anger issues. Some even suffered from hate and remorse, even though they would utter words like "love and light". Some of these friends were manipulative, controlling, conniving and mean to others – and I couldn't understand this conundrum for the life of me.

One day, while speaking to one of these friends on the phone and comparing notes about what we were experiencing, we came to the realization that something was messing with us. The deeper we got into the conversation, the more insight we got as to the culprit of our despair. We then decided to dig deeper and as we did, we uncovered something that many of us don't even want to talk about, something that we just touch upon when we go to the movies or read a book by one of our favorite horror authors – we were all the victims of forces that were dark, sinister and demonic.

The realization of what we were dealing with didn't sit well with me at all, but the more I researched and observed and interviewed "experts" in this field, the clearer the picture became. I didn't like what I was seeing, or what this implicated for humanity. Even worse was the fact that many of these New-Agers had been lured into a new religion that wasn't what it claimed to be. Many of them were folks that could have been instrumental in helping lift the consciousness of humanity, but instead were too busy working on themselves and their potential entry into Nirvana, to help anyone.

And then it hit me. The New Age Movement had been pre-planned. It was an agenda of the Sinister Forces to recruit those with the potential to uplift humanity, and render them ineffective. The new recruits would not be able to carry out the plan of bringing the balance designed by the Original Blueprint of Prime Creator back to this realm. It was a tactic, a strategy used by a very skillful enemy – one that knows the territory and has studied humanity and those that serve God/Creator. They know exactly how we behave and react, and so they have formulated a plan to capture as many of the ones that are "key players" and take them out of play. I then realized that what I was witnessing were battles being fought in the etheric or spiritual realm – battles springing from a very ancient and long-lasting Spiritual War.

Seeing so many New-Agers in distress revealed the pattern of their demise. There was a signature, a footprint left in the "spiritual sand" that one could trace right back to a culprit. And just like they had studied us, knew us better than we know ourselves through our predictable behavior, I was able to do the same. When I learned to read their "signature", I uncovered what was responsible for the mess humanity was in, and I was able to put a stop to their interfering in my personal life. My aim is to prevent them from interfering in your life as well so that you too can be instrumental in making a difference in this world and help others attain freedom. May this book provide you the Truth you seek and may it serve you well.

INTRODUCTION

1 Corinthians 3:16-17

"Do you not know that you are God's temple and that God's Spirit dwells in you? If anyone destroys God's temple, God will destroy him. For God's temple is holy, and you are that temple."

I think it is safe to say that things are not exactly in alignment with God's plan right now. The evidence of this is right under our noses. It could be as simple as an altercation between friends or the ill will you send to someone who cuts you off in traffic. It can be as grave as children being kidnaped and raped or murdered and the type of vileness that leads to beheadings and other atrocities. These are clear indications that something has been festering – something that could have been quashed by the Light Forces currently present but were instead left to grow like a cancer. This "thing" or Force is alive and has a consciousness. It is a beast without a body and with many bodies. It infests, enslaves and consumes. It is competent, it is wise, and it is unified. It has found our weaknesses – and it shows no mercy.

Because of this, we are facing unprecedented conditions on this plane of existence. The planet that was once ours has been inadvertently handed over to those acting on the Dark Force's behalf, to do with as they will. And they have been doing it unfettered, because those who were sent in to help correct this have themselves been severely compromised. These Forces are devouring God's Creation in this realm, and there's no one minding the store.

Make no mistake, this is a war – a spiritual war for the souls of man and womankind. It is a war to protect all that is holy and noble and good and innocent. It is a war to stop the defiling of all that is pure – like children and nature. Many of those who swore allegiance with The Light have either been taken out or have changed sides. However, there are others who have not yet been compromised and who are trying to get the rest to see that what is happening on Earth right now is not part of the Original Blueprint of Prime Creator.

I am urged to share the information in this book with as many souls that are willing to entertain it. This information may sound foreign at first, especially if you come from a traditional religion. Similarly, if you have not been practicing spirituality or are unfamiliar with New Age concepts, you may find the concepts a bit challenging to understand. But if you stick it out and keep reading, you'll find that your soul recognizes much of it. It is like starting to work out again after a long hiatus from the gym – your muscles will begin to remember.

Still others have been so immersed in the New Age philosophy and concepts that they are unwilling to let go of misguided beliefs, even when presented with Truth. They are fearful that their "enlightenment" will be shaken off its foundation. If you recognize yourself in this scenario, know that this too is a sign of being compromised by the Forces I address and expose in this book. True spiritual enlightenment can never be shaken or threatened by other viewpoints. Although many have come to the conclusion that we *do not* have free will on this planet, we do. So, you can opt to continue "blissing out" – New Age lingo for denial – so that you don't have to see what is actually happening around you; or, you can honor your responsibility to find what is causing the demise of such a beautiful world and all the living things in it.

If you have already claimed responsibility and would like to know what is causing us to experience pandemic entropy, death, despair, grief, and hopelessness, then the information contained in this book will help give you that understanding. If you are interested in empowering yourself to stand up with your fellow Light Emissaries and reclaim your Divine Power and Authority, you will find the strength to do so in this book.

It is my aim to awaken those who are being interfered with by Forces working in direct opposition to The Light and The Original Intention of Prime Creator. And time is of the essence, because of the urgency of the situation on this planet and because of how severely the Light Forces have been compromised. It is for everyone who is sick and tired of not being able to express their fullest potential, and is ready to throw off the shackles of this Matrix. Ultimately, this book is about us taking back our power and taking back our world – by returning the Kingdom of God into this realm.

To do this, we must first recognize the threat – for if we don't know what is causing an illness, how can we fight it? My aim is to pull back the curtain and reveal what is happening behind the scenes as we go to work, struggle to pay our bills, fight health problems, deal with divorces, go through depression, get heartbroken, and go through all of life's dramas.

While reading this book it is important to suspend all judgment and view it instead from a point of neutrality. If you rely on your intellect, you will find yourself arguing against the concepts because you don't want to let go of the old information – information that may be keeping you in bondage. Instead, try to approach it with the humility and awe of a little child, an empty vessel to be filled. This way, you give it the opportunity to be recognized by your soul. It may not resonate today, but it could tomorrow, as you start noticing the subtle deception that is occurring in your everyday reality – deception that usually portrays itself as information meant to liberate you. The realization of how we're deceived will be the beginning of your path to freedom.

You may also find that you already know much of this information. You may have heard it somewhere else, or it's already in the collective unconscious. If you are familiar with the concepts presented, please keep reading. You may be surprised that the way I tell this story may be unlike anything you've heard up to now, and it may connect a few more dots for you. Please give the book the chance to make its case and present the entire material.

Also, I have intentionally capitalized certain words to emphasize their importance and/or to differentiate them between the concepts and truths emanating from the Higher Realms and those found in this low-vibrational reality – also known as the third dimension. I have also included a Glossary of some terms that may be unfamiliar to you; the definitions are based on how I use them in the book. Finally, if this information does touch you on a soul level, be ready to act in service of others. It can be as simple as sharing what you've learned so that they too may begin to reexamine their lives and beliefs. The more of us who get inspired to take action, the quicker we'll restore the Will of God/Prime Creator to this world, raising the consciousness and vibration of humanity beyond all preconceived limits and expectations.

Only Breath — *Jelaluddin Rumi*
(translated by Coleman Barks)

*"Not Christian or Jew or Muslim, not Hindu
Buddhist, Sufi, or Zen. Not any religion
or cultural system. I am not from the East
or the West, not out of the ocean or up
from the ground, not natural or ethereal, not
composed of elements at all. I do not exist,
am not an entity in this world or the next,
did not descend from Adam and Eve or any
origin story. My place is placeless, a trace
of the traceless. Neither body or soul.
I belong to the beloved, have seen the two
worlds as one and that one call to and know,
first, last, outer, inner, only that
breath breathing human being."*

PART I

WHO ARE WE?

CHAPTER 1

EARTH EXPERIENCE

"It is divinity that shapes, not only your ends, but also your acts,
your words and thoughts."

—Swami Sivananda

It's time to have a meaningful talk about our current experience on this planet. We like to tell ourselves that the world is like a magnificent painting, composed of a multitude of colors and textures that would please just about anyone. Yet what is really manifesting in this world, and the reality of what many people are in fact experiencing in their lives, paints an entirely different picture – and it is no masterpiece. It's time to get real.

Now, it is possible that you may be having a fantastic experience here – one full of enjoyment and fulfillment. But, if you're like most folks, you're probably experiencing something quite different. If you're like me, you've already seen things that just don't make any sense – like the disparity between classes in any given society; the mistreatment of women and the elderly; the taking away of lands from indigenous people, genocide, fabricated wars and the abuse of children, animals and the environment. If you're like me, you may have already asked yourselves, "If there's a God, how can there be so much cruelty in this world?" If you're like me, you may have wondered why, despite being a good person who loves the The Supreme, Prime Creator and has shown It a tremendous amount of faith and loyalty, you are experiencing hardship, loneliness, conflict with others, illnesses, despair, abuse, fear, and financial insecurity.

You know you've done everything right – you're a Good Samaritan, you respect all life, you pray or meditate; you go to work, pay your bills and pay your taxes; you try to look at the brighter side of life, yet it seems like those that worship money and materialistic things thrive and appear to live abundant, healthy and somewhat happy lives. By now, if you're like me, you may have arrived at the conclusion that there is something wrong with this picture. It's a world that doesn't make sense – a world that favors those that glorify the "Golden Calf", as opposed to those that praise God. What is manifesting in this world today is the antithesis of Godliness; it is a defiling of the Divine Plan. And if we've come to this conclusion, we must surely agree that something has gone awry, and something is helping to fuel the chaos.

You wake up every day, hoping something different will happen – something magical that will give you hope, or a renewed faith that things will change for the better. But it doesn't; instead, you're feeling like you're in the movie "Ground Hog Day" – your life is a repetition of what is not working. Then you may get a sick feeling inside when you realize that you're stuck in this world, at least for now, and in a body that you may not even like that much or doesn't work right much of the time. You go to work every day because you have no choice, or you don't work because you can't, or there are no jobs that will hire you. And you're tired. You're tired of the struggle to live. You want to know how the story ends, and you want to know what the exit strategy is – or if there's even an exit strategy.

You may conclude that your entire life is one big test, or you're on a mission of some sort, but you were never given a job manual or a job description. You were just told to show up – no instructions provided. You watch the terrible things on the news and yearn for a world of eternal peace and bliss and unconditional love – a world that exists when unifying with God. You may be holding on to the hope of a Rapture or Ascension. You find yourself asking, "Why am I even here? What is my purpose and what is expected of me?"

I too know all these feelings well. I have been obsessed with finding the reason I was sent to this chaotic place. I am beyond tired of being in "The Matrix" – otherwise known as "The Prison" or "The Truman Show" or a sadistic Alien software program that keeps us enslaved. What you and I are both looking for is our freedom from an experience that is a bit trite and not what we expected.

Being "free" means many things to different people. What I refer to here is freedom from the life-death cycle; freedom from all limitations; freedom from health issues; freedom from interpersonal drama; freedom from pain, suffering and fear; freedom from strife and freedom from this lower-density world, and all the physics and not-so-pleasant entities that govern it. I could probably write a book just on the different kinds of bleak conditions and situations that humanity needs to be freed from. What we do not realize is that the roadmap to this freedom is already inside us. It isn't conveniently purchased at the local gas station. It is innately ours. I know that you know how to achieve this freedom. You have done this before in other lifetimes and in other worlds that you've "chosen" to experience. The problem is the knowledge may be dormant within you because of the amnesia that was placed over each one of us, otherwise known as the veil.

You harbor the complete memory of your soul's origin, and it is from this memory that the feelings of "homesickness" arise. Every now and again you get this sense of "Knowing" another, very different place; moreover, you still feel attached to it as if through some invisible, Cosmic Umbilical Cord. Your place of origin is more than likely a High-Vibratory Realm, a place many call The Higher Heavens or The Kingdom of God, but in reality it could be a myriad of different High-Vibratory worlds. You know the sensation of being there very well, and it differs significantly from what you experience here. Those vague memories confirm for you the notion that you're not from this density – originally. You then may find yourself being very impatient in this realm and a bit disappointed of what the experience has turned out to be.

These Realms or planes of existence are also in service to bring The Will of Prime Creator to all Creation. These Realms express in states of Perfection, Beauty, Bliss, Truth, Balance, Harmony, Peace, Radiance and Eternal Love. These states of Perfection resonate with most of us because it is embedded in our soul's memory bank, and we spend our life in this embodiment seeking to have these experiences again. It is what drives us. Without this longing, our life would be banal – to put it kindly.

You may already have had a glimpse of these Realms of Perfection, most likely during a spiritually, transformational experience. It could have happened when going to church and experiencing a sublime moment there, or when in prayer and contemplation, or during a meditation that connected you with The All That Is. Whichever way it has happened for you – if it has – you were propelled into a momentary state of bliss, a feeling of eternal peace or overwhelming, unconditional love. Unfortunately, the experience may have been short-lived, especially if you were distracted by the mundane: thinking that you had to cook dinner, or answer the phone, or pay the bills. You were brought right back to this reality.

This reality is comprised of low density, which in turn equates to solid matter. The sensation of this low-density reality is similar to moving through quicksand and having weights tied around your waist and limbs. The feeling of density provides a sharp contrast with the worlds you come from originally. These worlds are filled with magnificent, radiant colors. Light permeates everything – it has a consciousness and is alive. The experiences there are Joyful, Peaceful, and Harmonious. And the feeling of Oneness with all Creation is expressed via the Glorious Music that plays unceasingly, as a way to exalt the Creator. You may even have memories of being weightless, of flying, of traveling using your intention and manifesting out of thin air. This enhanced state of being is a big contrast to what you're currently experiencing and where you are physically at this moment… Here, it's a different ballgame altogether.

If you're like most of the beings who originate from those Realms, I'm sure your goal is to get back to those states of bliss and perfection – why wouldn't it be? This is why so many of us embark on a spiritual quest, why we've sought out religious and spiritual leaders, teachers and gurus, and we've made efforts to connect with spiritual guides and indigenous elders. We all carry that hope in our heart that those that we seek out, whom we believe are "connected" with Truth, can provide us with the roadmap that will lead us to our "Return Home" – our True Home.

Because you have soul memory of these Higher Worlds or states of existence, you have already attained a spiritual level that has enabled your vibration to be of the same frequency as that of those Realms. Your essence, in other words, is of High-Vibratory origin – of Mastery! It is the only way you can reside in such Realms and, therefore, have memories of them. To achieve this high vibration requires great spiritual attainment. Therefore, you already reached that level of spiritual-proficiency *before* you incarnated on Earth!

So you see, Mastery is inherent in you. If you pay close attention, becoming "in tune" with whom you really are, and if you begin to function from your inner "Knowing", you'll realize that you have all that you need to achieve that level of Mastery again and go beyond it. The key here is to remember how to access this knowledge "at will", which will also allow you to reclaim your Mastery in this Lower-Density Realm.

This lifetime then becomes a great opportunity for spiritual growth, if you choose to see it as such. The task and *one* of the reasons you embodied on this planet, is to re-acquire and surpass your Mastery level, despite the challenges and the odds, despite the hurdles and the limitations, despite the density, ugliness and darkness that manifests in the outer world. We are to do this despite the so-called "evil" governments, greedy corporations and the Sinister Forces that have taken over this world. This assignment, if you choose to accept it, is to transcend all of it and soar above it; it also entails helping others achieve the same thing.

This tapping into your dormant "Master within" usually happens when you're "in-tune" with the Divine Spark that dwells in all of us. It takes dedication. It takes practice. It takes perseverance. It takes patience. You have to tap into that inner Master in every world you chose to embody in. If you don't, you become aimless, with no direction; you're like a buoy in the vast ocean of life, with the waves of circumstance and unique challenges steering you in different directions. Without a navigational system or map, you end up exactly where you started or much worse – bashed against sharp rocks.

Each low-vibratory world and experience are different. They possess various obstacles and challenges. Each one has its set of Negative-Polarity Overseers or administrators whose role is to maintain a level of density via low-vibrational acts and experiences. They do this by creating havoc, strife, despair, hopelessness, doubt, pain and fear. These conditions pose challenges that ultimately elicit "choices". When you continuously make choices that are in alignment with the Divine Will of God, you achieve your next level of spiritual attainment – that gets you closer to the "Return."

CHALLENGES AND OUR MASTERY

Imagine if you will an athlete who is running the mile. He crosses the finish line in three minutes and a half, breaking the world record and winning the Gold Medal. Next year he competes again, only this time, another athlete manages to run the mile in three-and-a-quarter minutes, breaking the record and winning the Gold. The former winner, in his training, might have taken into consideration the fact that he was a year older. He could have been mindful that the terrain was probably different and that the humidity would be a factor in the new place of competition. He should have had the foresight that the other athletes might be training harder to beat his record and win. He should have practiced with these things in mind, in order to prepare himself for the challenge.

Spiritual Mastery is similar in that the "Gold Medal" is representative of your maximum achievement or the attainment that is possible for you in any given lifetime. In one particular life, in a particular world, you may attain the "Gold", and in the next you may have a whole new set of circumstances and challenges. You will have to exercise your spiritual muscle to be "at the top of your game" there, in order to win the top prize – your Spiritual Mastery.

One of the fringe benefits you get via your Mastery (which is Self-Mastery and Spiritual-Mastery), is breaking free of the life-death cycle. Some other benefits are becoming eternally youthful; having perpetual, vibrant health and breaking free from the confines of density. Other important ones are shattering the illusion of limitation; stepping out of the rules of lower-density physics;

being impervious to Lower-Dimensional Overlords, and not having to adhere to third-dimensional time or space. It also gives you so much more. It provides you with Self-Realization and ultimately God-Realization.

Mastery of anything, especially in this world, comes at a price. In our society, there is usually some kind of financial investment involved, and an investment of time, commitment and discipline. College is a great example – it requires a significant expenditure of both money and time. If you invest the money but don't put in the time and dedication, you probably won't know the material well enough to get high grades. Perhaps they'll be good enough for graduation, but this is still mediocrity, not mastery, of the material. Not mastering the material means you won't have the knowledge required to be as competent in your chosen field. Of course, not being proficient in the subject matter could also mean you didn't graduate at all – a total waste of your time and money.

Reacquiring your Spiritual Mastery seems easy, in theory – of course it would, it's in your memory bank. Putting this knowledge into practice, however, is another thing altogether. It's like climbing Mt. Everest barefoot, with no gear – it is a challenge beyond all challenges. But you try regardless because you want to "Return Home" to the Bosom of God, so you aim at reaching the higher levels of spiritual attainment in this embodiment. You begin by being careful not to harm others and to be in unity consciousness most of the time. You become conscious of what foods to eat and how everything is energy and interconnected. You begin to pray more or meditate; you go on spiritual journeys and spiritual gatherings. These things make you feel connected to others and the planet. You are making great spiritual progress, so you think.

The real test is whether you're still struggling with issues of anger, doubt, resentment, gossip, jealousy, hate, fear, being egotistical and judgmental, etc. If you are displaying any of these behaviors or emotions, you will be hindered in reaching your highest spiritual potential. So, yes, you may have crossed the finish line, but didn't get the "spiritual" Gold, the Silver or even the Bronze. You didn't "master" yourself for the task at hand. In short, you missed the mark – your goal of winning first-place.

Yes, you can always enter another race and train harder so that you win the top prize the next time around. And that is what many of us do in an embodiment. When we "miss the mark", we're given the opportunity to try again – not necessarily as in a reincarnation, but as another incarnation or expression with other challenges that also require Mastering or proficiency.

What many of us are seeking in this incarnation is the human experience, with all the opportunities and challenges that come with it. This embodiment is a unique opportunity that may not present itself again, at least, not in the way it's presenting itself to us who are here now. So taking advantage of it, being cognizant of what it takes to come out with the Gold Medal has to be a priority and a commitment that you're willing and ready to make.

By now you have a sense that you have a much greater purpose than just getting up every day and going to work. You know your existence means more than just paying bills, paying taxes, getting the latest car, remodeling your home or going on vacation. You are "awake" enough to realize that there is something more to life than doing the hamster-on-the-wheel thing.

You may have come to the realization that there is something greater than the hardships so prevalent on this plane of existence. After enduring the loss or betrayal of friends; the loss of loved ones; financial devastation or the loss of your health, becoming bitter, jaded, and cynical is very typical. It isn't uncommon to build walls around yourself to prevent experiencing any more suffering. Sometimes you'll feel so defeated from all these experiences that you don't have the strength to continue trying.

Sometimes you'll feel like you're spiraling downward into an abyss, where there is no hope. Too exhausted to continue fighting, you become consumed by negativity and low-vibratory thoughts and emotions. It is at this moment, when things look their bleakest, that you get to make the choice. You may decide to give up and hit the bottom of the abyss, or you can choose to flap your wings as hard as you can and fly out of it. "Flying out" means you decided to take control of your life. You've decided that you are the captain of your ship – your "body-vehicle". At this point, you might ask for guidance and spiritual help. You may fall on your knees in surrender. You may begin to pray to a God you've known about, dismissed at some point in your life, and now feel the need to connect with again – because nothing else is working.

It is in this attempt to connect to God, Prime Creator, or whatever name you know "It" by, that change begins to occur. It happens because your ego is out of the way. It finally dawns on you that you are ephemeral and vulnerable and can't overcome these challenges on your own. You somehow manage to humble yourself and approach God "as a little child" – in awe and wonder... And you find that this actually works, and you establish communication. You enter into communion with the Creator in this manner because you have left the mind out of the picture and engaged your heart. It is through your heart that you communicate with Prime Creator and no other way. It happens when you surrender to the moment, become an empty vessel, and allow this exchange to take place.

THE OPPORTUNITIES

I have had numerous challenges in my life, but some of the most difficult occurred after my divorce, when I was trying to support my young children. I remember being so relieved when I got a job paying a substantial amount of money, and how devastated I was when I lost it. With this job, I had finally been able to live comfortably and take care of my kids. I was also living beyond my means because I thought the money and the position would be permanent. When they laid me off, I was in a state of shock. I came home that day in a zombie-like fashion – spiritually, mentally, emotionally and physically numb.

When it finally hit me, I sunk into a deep depression and cried every night. I was too hurt and too angry to think clearly. Every day, I looked in the newspaper for a job, and I attracted nothing. I had a victim mentality and sometimes I couldn't get out of bed. The bills were piling up, the mortgage was due, and the food was running out. I didn't see a light at the end of the tunnel. I was tailspinning.

One day a well-meaning friend asked me to go with her to a Home Expo – she was trying to get me out of the house. It took a little convincing on her part, but I finally said I would go. There were all kinds of vendors at the event; they had set up tables and were selling their products and services. I noticed a mortgage company giving out information, and I walked right over to them. I asked what it would take to get a second mortgage on my house so I could pull out some money. They answered my questions; I filled out an application, and in a few weeks I had obtained a second mortgage on my home. It was the first glimmer of hope in months.

I used the funds to set up my own business, and while it didn't bring in a lot of money, it was enough to pay the bills. It also bought me time to explore another industry – one that was very lucrative at the time – the mortgage business. Before long, I became one of the top mortgage executives in the company and was catapulted to a level of financial success that I didn't' even know was possible.

I realized that if I hadn't been laid off, feeling much internal pain and self-doubt, I never would have thought out of the box and gone into an entirely different industry. Being placed in uncomfortable situations got me to explore another side of myself, one that was talented and very successful – a winner. I attained another level of expertise and another level of financial rewards that equated to peace of mind, joy and self-worth. I had risen out of the ashes, just like a phoenix.

So, how do you deal with the experience of physical, mental, emotional and/or spiritual pain? Some of us don't deal with it at all; we just live with it, thinking it's just a part of our life – "the way things are". Others will seek ways to alleviate the symptoms, like one does when taking aspirin – without addressing the actual cause of the problem. And some of us will take the opportunity to use these experiences as a springboard for spiritual and personal growth.

Let's talk for a moment about those that decide to see negative experiences as gifts in disguise. Say, for example, that you have anxiety about a situation. It keeps you awake at night and is causing a lot of emotional, mental and spiritual pain and turmoil. You could choose to transcend the negative experience by 1) tapping into your innate Mastery skills that will help you navigate out of the situation or painful experience, 2) transcend the painful experience by becoming still and listening to your inner voice – which gives you the insight necessary to know how to correct the situation, 3) make a direct connection with Creator, where the channel of communication is established and all solutions are provided, 4) use protection and shielding techniques that will protect you, make you invisible to negative energy and transmute the situation into a positive one. (These concepts and techniques can be found in my other book, *Getting Back to Source: Tools for Connection, Protection & Empowerment*.)

You also have a fifth option: do nothing. It means that you ignore the above opportunities to connect with Source-Creator and exercise your Spiritual Mastery. You can decide that whatever is hurting you is too big to tackle and that God never hears you anyway, so you become more bitter and angry. Options one through four are the opportunities to change the negative circumstance by consciously choosing to do so. Option five is the path that most people take because the others require work and most people have no more fight left in them. They are done.

Remembering who you are is crucial to understanding that you can Master all the negative experiences in your life. When you start flexing your spiritual muscle and retraining yourself for Spiritual Mastery, you will acquire the know-how to overcome the *super challenges* and *overwhelming obstacles* that are evident in the outer world. Many of these challenges come in the form of social conditions like inequality, hate crimes, injustices, and prejudices. Then there are more severe conditions like contamination of the Earth, wars, exploitation of women and children, and the atrocities against all life. You cannot fix monumental situations when you have no control over the situations and drama in your own life. So, knowing how to Master yourself should be your first and most important task at this moment. In order to begin doing this, it is important to remember who you truly are.

CHAPTER 2

REMEMBERING WHO YOU ARE

"The rose is a rose from the time it is a seed to the time it dies. Within it, at all times, it contains its whole potential. It seems to be constantly in the process of change: Yet at each state, at each moment, it is perfectly all right as it is."

—**Paulo Coelho, "Warrior of the Light"**

From the age of four, I have vivid memories of a Realm of Perfection, a Realm of perpetual Joy, Peace, and Beauty. At that young age, I am communicating with Prime Creator and the Higher Realms and Councils that serve God/Prime Creator. I begin taking off my shoes and kneeling by my bedside, in a gesture of humility to communicate with The All That Is. I am not taught to do this – I receive "downloads", or instantaneous information that starts to shape me and give me understandings about myself and the Realms I had come from originally. The information provided is not presented in a way that I can verbalize or logically put together. It sits in my soul's "memory bank" – so to speak – and I pull from this endless resource of information as I need to.

Many times I use techniques that would normally be considered magic in this world. The techniques are just a part of the gifts that we are all privy to in the Illumined Worlds or Realms of Prime Creator. Because I remember these gifts, I begin to heal myself and others. I also create positive situations for myself and my family and turn negative situations into loving and peaceful outcomes for all involved.

I never have a need to understand why or how this works – I just know it does. So whenever I want to change an outcome, I use these techniques. When I want to make myself invisible – while being in a room with others – I use the techniques that I still remember from the Higher Realms. When I want to become extremely strong and powerful, I become strong and powerful because I know how to do this, as it is part of my being and the fabric of my soul.

I have done this so many times before this embodiment that it is natural to me. At age four, I know that I can operate in this manner. I am not yet aware that this isn't normal in most people. I comprehend that I am allowed to receive information from the Higher Worlds and to remember that I am not originating from this world. Later in life, I realize that the memory of my gifts occurred because I was partially veiled – allowing me to remember some things, but not all.

The most disturbing aspect of this partial veil is a terrible feeling of homesickness due to vivid memories of my real home. Because I remember many things from The Higher Realms, the sense of being trapped in my physical body becomes more pronounced. I am aware of the many restrictions that come with being in a body. I know that I'm in a very dense realm, yet my soul still feels very expansive and can do anything. This dichotomy causes me confusion and great internal pain.

WE BRING OUR SKILLS

The experience of taking embodiment is similar to getting into your car and going to your job. Just because you go to work doesn't mean you sever the ties to your home, your family and who you truly are. Your true self is the "real you" that you are when you return home after the workday is done. When you're at home, you operate with ease because you are familiar with your surroundings and the intricacies of running your household. You are, for the most part, more relaxed and in the driver's seat because you're not playing out a role that is required (i.e. your job description). When you go to work each day, you bring with you a desire – to complete the day's task so you can go back home again and be yourself, be in your familiar surroundings. You also bring your innate talents and skills to do that job. You are already knowledgeable, experienced and gifted before you even enter the office, and you acquire more skills through your experience at the job.

Similarly, you are here now working in whatever capacity and having a human experience at this moment. But the Higher expression of you knows Home and longs to return. So, with this in mind, and as I was saying in the previous chapter, a Master dwells within you; you already have all you need to be that again, and more. But also remember that this type of attainment requires an absolute command over your physical, mental and emotional bodies. Each one of these must be subjugated. If you have supremacy on all but one, it keeps you from completing your Mastery. It is similar in concept to passing all your college courses except one – and all were necessary for graduation. There is a reason to believe that without having passed the courses necessary for graduation, you will not receive your college diploma or move to the next level in your studies or career.

You have dwelled in the Realms of Truth, Bliss, Balance, Harmony, Peace and Love before, and you recognize this experience as being natural for you. If you're like me, you yearn to acquire this state of existence again. This yearning is what propels you and me towards our spiritual path here on planet Earth. And it is this desire and need to return to those perfect and sublime states of existence that makes us seek truth from different sources. But, the seeking of "any" kind of information just for the sake of obtaining information, especially if it gives us an instantaneous rush or "spiritual high", is not beneficial.

Information-overindulgence has been what has kept a lot of us from connecting with the Higher Realms that we are so fervently seeking. This hunger we have for knowledge – knowledge that will help us make sense of the world we live in; or the path our life has taken; or how to return to our real home – needs to be appropriately guided in order to use the energy of this desire to achieve its maximum potential. If we don't, it could make the journey back home almost impossible to accomplish or unnecessarily delayed.

MY THREE CENTS OF WHO YOU ARE

So who are you, really? Like the thimble that is dipped into the ocean and now contains a sample of sea water, similarly, you contain all the ingredients of Prime Creator. The thimble-full of sea water contains all the elements and molecules of the ocean, yet it is not the ocean in its entirety and complexity. This concept holds true for you as well, as you would not be the Creator in Its entirety and complexity. When you reconnect yourself with Source or Prime Creator, you reacquire the Totality of Its Divine Essence again; it's like bathing in the ocean as opposed to pouring the thimble-full of sea water over you. When you "Return Home" to Source-Prime-Creator, it is similar to pouring the thimble-full of sea water back into the Ocean. The water sample will automatically become part of the ocean all over again and can now be called Ocean.

The Creator or Source simply is. It is *Every* "thing" and *No* "thing". It is Love, Light, Bliss, Beginningless, Endless, Harmonious, Balanced, Shapeless, Nameless and Eternal. It is "The All That Is", "The All That Was" and "The All That Shall Be". It is Prime and Supreme. One of the ways that Creator expresses Itself is via Sound, especially through the Audible Life Stream or the Sound Current (explained further in *Getting Back to Source: Tools for Connection, Protection & Empowerment*). Also, all of Creation is made up of vibration. The vibration is the vibration of Prime Creator. It is the ultimate vibratory rate experienced at Zero Point. What is Zero Point? For the purpose of this book, it is the unification of The All – the created and Creator as One! It is that state of Perfection, of Balance or Harmony or Homeostasis where everything is in Balance and a perpetual state of "Isness."

A CREATION THEORY

Prime Creator manifests Its Creations by compression of Itself. In other words, It lowers that perfect vibratory level in order to slow down the electronic movement just enough to begin to create different vibratory Realms. Each Realm is progressively of a lower vibration. Picture those Russian nesting dolls called Babushkas, where each wooden doll nests within another. If we could see these newly created Realms, they too would similarly be nested in this manner. The ones with the highest frequency would form the outer layers and the ones with the lowest would nest inside.

Then, Beings of Supreme Luminosity and Intelligence would be created to reside within these Higher-Vibrational Realms to manifest universes and worlds of their own. Those that are of the Highest-Vibratory-Level would occupy the Realms closest to Prime Creator. These Beings would be known as Creator "gods" and would emulate Prime Creator by carrying out Its Divine Plan. Part of that plan is to create worlds that become populated by a myriad of life-forms and intelligent life that eventually seek their return to Zero Point.

EXPERIENCING LIKE CREATOR

Let's try a quick exercise. Sit quietly for a moment, in an armchair, with your bare feet touching the floor, and your eyes closed. Feel the chair with both hands. Let your fingers explore the texture of the chair; feel the temperature of the surface and the nuances of the fabric. Do the same with your feet and your toes, feeling the floor. Is the floor smooth or bumpy? Is the floor cold, damp, textured? Each toe should be exploring the floor. As the central "presence" or "being" processing this information, your job is to take in all the experiences that your extremities are having, while you sit in the chair.

Each one of these extremities, especially your fingers and toes, are independently having an experience. These experiences may be similar or unique. Each extremity then reports back to you, so that you can make sense of the surroundings. You take in the information that will provide you with a clear understanding of your present reality. This information is collected by you, via the extensions of yourself.

The limbs or extremities are not you, but a part of you. You are experiencing your immediate world – the chair and the floor – by animating these extremities, which are representatives of you, but not you in your totality. You infuse them with your life-force and intelligence, and you allow them to feel, to explore, to experience. They in turn respond and give Intel back to you. Similarly, but in a more complex way, God/Creator does the same with Its Creation.

THE PLAN

The goal of The Plan is to allow the varied expressions of Prime Creator to "Return Home" through their free will, by making the choice to do so. The Return Home is the Joy of The Supreme God. It is similar to birthing a child, raising it till it's mature enough to take care of itself, and hoping that it will come home every so often to ask your advice. The desire of Prime Creator is to witness Its Creation returning back to Itself.

The Supreme God facilitates the proliferation of intelligent life on pre-selected worlds, and it's in these worlds where this intelligence will ultimately face embodiment challenges. Prime Creator observes Its Creation by becoming the Creation; and, as Creator, It waits for the moment when Its Creation returns to Itself. Again, it's like the thimbleful of ocean water returning to the vast ocean once again. Those intelligent life-forms that were placed in these worlds as Sparks of The Divine will hopefully remember that they have the Essence of The Supreme and that they are part of the Whole. Once that realization occurs, then their spiritual quest begins – a journey that aims to reconnect their life-stream back into the vastness of the Cosmic Ocean.

Reconnecting to Source is necessary to allow the Creator-Essence, in its entirety, to flow back through the "Cosmic Umbilical Cord", allowing the flow of God-Particles and God-Essence to mingle with our life-stream. This exposure to Divine-Essence is why continuous connection to Source or Prime Creator, and the constant influx of Source-Particles and God-Attributes makes the life-stream act, live and breathe Source. Being immersed in the presence of God is how a life-stream or the expression of you emulates Source-Creator in this current embodiment.

Intelligent life, like humanity, is given the opportunity to evolve spiritually by being presented with challenges that are aimed to force choices. A life-expression's spiritual maturity comes into play as it determines what decisions will be made with respect to the challenges imposed on their physical, mental and emotional bodies. Based on the choices, the being or expression will either raise its consciousness and vibration, or lower it. The higher the consciousness and vibration, the closer it gets to "The Return."

THE ONLY CONNECTION TO MAKE

You may have already met and surpassed all the challenges that were imposed on you in all the worlds that you've chosen an embodiment. So, you may have already Mastered the physical, mental and emotional limitations – a prerequisite for attaining Self-Mastery. This level of spiritual attainment has not been effortless. It never is. You probably had to jump enormous hurdles, starting with controlling your emotional body, cleansing and purifying your thought processes, being in service to others and expressing Christ consciousness. You've also had to sustain this Mastery long enough to accelerate your vibration to the highest potential that you could achieve, in order to enter and stay in those Illumined Realms that are the closest to the Bosom of Prime Creator. Therefore, "Mastery" is inherent in you and in all who embodied in a dense world in order to uphold the Light and to restore the "Will of God."

The God that I am referring to here is Prime Creator. It is the Creator of All That is, and the Creator of all the lesser Creator "gods", and all their universes. It is this God, whom the Hebrews refer to as the Hashem or the Abba Nartoomid, the Father of the Eternal Light. Many ancient texts provide accounts of Beings that have come to a world like Earth in order to seed it with life-forms or accelerate evolution. These are the demiurges or lesser gods, or extraterrestrial intelligence that has been revered as gods. Regardless of what alien race or lesser god helped in manipulating our genetics, the only Being we need to connect with is Prime Creator.

Connection to The All That Is – Source/Prime Creator – is imperative for those of us seeking our way back Home. The Journey Home is laborious and one that doesn't seem to end; the aim is getting back to Zero Point. It is a process. All Beings of Light, who dwell in the Higher Heavens, go through the same process of spiritual evolution as everything in Creation spirals upward, in vibration and consciousness, towards this attainment.

The goal now should be to 1) remember who you are, 2) rekindle your "Knowing" about your spiritual attainments, 3) reclaim your Divine Power & Authority, 4) become a proactive member of Earth, 5) be instrumental in bringing about change by helping to uplift the current consciousness on Earth, and 6) attain your Christ/God-Consciousness. If you don't focus on achieving these things, you will have had another corporal experience, albeit a wonderful one, that may not have made the kind of impact that you envisioned for yourself before embodiment. Of course, you may not even remember what you had envisioned before embodiment – but for those that do, being on task is crucial, especially considering the times we're in.

In order to achieve these goals, you need to have an acute awareness and get in-tune with your Divine Powers. Achieving the above doesn't happen by simply having a desire to be spiritual and wanting to go back Home. It takes work and effort. I'm pretty sure you understand by now that nothing worth acquiring or attaining falls into our lap – if it does we wouldn't value it, and we'd all be there already! Something that is of this magnificence has a price. The Kingdom of Heaven, as is known in the Bible, Zero Point, The Bosom of God, Unity, or The Return is where we need to maintain our focus. It's going to take diligent and daily communion, contemplation, direct communication, and infusion with the Mind and Heart of God. Without this, Christ or God Consciousness is not possible because the earthly or mundane aspects of life on Earth will pull you to denser consciousness and lower vibratory experiences. It is only through this infusion with Mind and Heart of God that we gain Self-Mastery and our freedom from the lower densities.

Freedom from all lower-density conditions is one of the prizes that all Light Emissaries who serve Prime Creator strive for. To do this, we must acquire the level of Mastery necessary to raise our consciousness and our vibratory level to the highest octave possible. As I said earlier, achieving this Mastery takes great discipline, but once we have it we start moving up the rungs of the ladder – closer and closer with each attempt at entering Zero Point. How this is actualized in the physical, denser world is through the Connection with Source, which starts with our choice to connect.

Our choices, therefore, are paramount. The correct choices, those that move us forward, propelling us quickly towards raising our consciousness and vibration, are made possible only when adverse situations are faced and overcome. The truth is that nobody likes those challenging situations – and most of us don't believe they're necessary for our spiritual growth. We avoid these negative experiences at all costs. We'll explore this a bit more in future chapters, but for now, suffice it to say that one of the reasons we resist the negative experiences is because we've actually forgotten the reasons we're in this realm.

CHAPTER 3

OUR AMNESIA

"I shall remember while the light lives yet
And in the night time I shall not forget."
—From *Erotion* by Algeron Charles Swinburne

Here's an eye-opening concept: Prime Creator embraces Positive Polarity or Light, and also Negative Polarity or Darkness. The Positive Polarity (Light) expresses at the highest vibratory rate, whereas Negative Polarity (Darkness) takes on the lowest. Because Prime Creator contains *Every* "thing" and *No* "thing", It contains both. Negative Polarity helps those that want to "Return" by providing mechanisms that help in their return. This opportunity is given to all those who exhibit intelligence in any given world – in this case, planet Earth; however, not everyone will recognize this as an opportunity to exit the third-dimensional experience.

Many of those who come in already as "Masters" from Higher Realms, forget the purpose of the challenges provided by the

Negative Polarity aspect or Dark Forces. Instead, they spend most of the experience in a state of suffering and bitterness. They, unfortunately, have identified with the reality they are experiencing, forgetting the nature of Creator and the Plan, failing to remember their direct connection and their Divinity. They do not notice the opportunities that are presented, opportunities that act as springboards out of this third-dimensional experience.

So yes, there are "things" that are placed in a dense world, like this one, that serve the Negative-Aspect of Creator, and it's there on purpose. These adverse circumstances and experiences are set in place for the purpose of giving us hurdles, stumbling blocks and unpleasant experiences that force us to make choices. What kind of choices? Well, we can choose to react negatively to a situation, we can choose to stay objective, or we can choose to respond with love. These are the choices. The first one elicits negative energy and reacting with love elicits positive energy. Being objective or neutral conjures neither positive nor negative energy and allows you to be in a place of discernment. Choices that are in alignment with The Will of Prime Creator also serve to bring us balance, and this ripples into the Cosmos to add towards the balance there as well.

As much as you may not want to hear this, there is no growth without challenges of the Opposing Forces – none! The opportunity for challenges is why many times Beings that have already attained their Spiritual Mastery, and currently reside in Higher-Vibratory Realms, embody into a low-vibratory world. They do so in order to have the Opposing Forces push them into making the choices necessary to expand their consciousness further and raise their vibrations to an even higher level. They understand that they would not be able to achieve this without the negative influence.

Let's take a look at it from this perspective: in a Perfect World of Balance, where everything is in Harmony and all Beings get along – a world of Love and Light and Bliss – the Beings there will stay in that state perpetually, in Homeostasis, with nothing to push them up the next rung of the ladder. With this in mind, it's time for a little physics refresher. Right now, you may be asking what physics has to do with all of this, and the answer is: everything. For example, Isaac Newton's first law of motion states:

"An object at rest stays at rest and an object in motion stays in motion with the same speed and in the same direction unless acted upon by an unbalanced force."

In other words, left to themselves, objects don't speed up, don't slow down, and don't change direction, unless some outside force – that is unbalanced – acts on it. If they're at rest, they will stay at rest, in the same state, undisturbed. If they are in motion, with a particular direction and velocity, they will remain on this path and at this speed – unless an unbalanced force interferes to change that. In order to get a deeper understanding, we're going to define balanced and unbalanced forces.

EXAMPLE OF A BALANCED FORCE

Forces that are of equal strength or magnitude and going in opposite directions cancel each other out. So, this means that an object at rest that is being acted upon by two forces going in contrary directions and of equal magnitude will not move – the object will remain motionless. These forces also don't cause a change in motion. If the object is stable, it will remain stationary indefinitely. (See Figure 1)

Balanced Forces

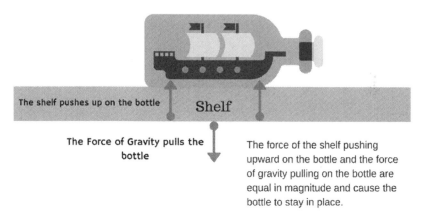

The shelf pushes up on the bottle **Shelf**

The Force of Gravity pulls the bottle

The force of the shelf pushing upward on the bottle and the force of gravity pulling on the bottle are equal in magnitude and cause the bottle to stay in place.

Bottle is Motionless (Equilibrium - Stagnation)

Figure 1

EXAMPLE OF AN UNBALANCED FORCE

These are unequal forces going in the opposite direction that do cause a change in motion, even if the object is stationary. Unbalanced Forces are important as these are what cause a motionless object to move. Also, if an object is already in motion and an Unbalanced Force acts on it, it causes its velocity to change and can affect its direction. If another Force enters the equation, like Friction, it can cause the object to not accelerate or slow it down. (See Figure 2)

Unbalanced Forces

Friction is another force that is now acting on the bottle, slowing down its speed.

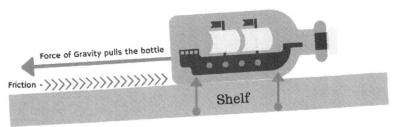

Force of Gravity pulls the bottle

Friction -

Shelf

The shelf pushes upward on the bottle

The bottle starts to move down the slope due to Unbalanced Forces acting on it. In this case, the force of gravity is greater due to the tilting of the shelf.

The Bottle is set into a slow, downward motion

Figure 2

In Figure 2, the bottle will be at rest or stagnant when the Balanced Forces are acting on it. But, if we tilt the shelf, the bottle will slide downward, set in motion by the force of gravity, which is now greater than the force that the shelf exerts on the bottle. Now the forces are unbalanced and the greater pull of gravity will make it move. The greater the incline, the faster it will slide down.

The diagram also shows the force of friction that will serve to slow down the bottle. Because the magnitude of the force of gravity is greater than the force of friction, in this case, the bottle will still move but the speed will be reduced. When no resistance is present, the bottle will move at a speed directly proportional to the degree of incline. It will continue this way indefinitely until something stops it, or another unbalanced force acts on it.

NEWTON'S LAW AND YOUR MASTERY

There are certain Universal Laws that can also be found in the laws of physics; however, unlike Newton's Laws, they work unilaterally and equally on all of God's Creation. They don't just apply to Earth or our Third-Dimensional Reality – they are Universal. With respect to Beings of Light that have already reached a level of spiritual achievement, this Law of Physics will explain why they make a conscious choice to embody in such a dense and low-vibratory world as is planet Earth.

In those beautiful worlds of Harmony, Bliss, Peace, Love, Balance, and Radiance, these Beings of Light will reside there, in these perfected states – perpetually. There is very little that happens, if anything at all, which will create the opportunity for the further advancement of their souls' evolution. There is nothing confronting them with challenges – nothing pushing them forward.

Many think that we have to be in "unity consciousness" and not in duality. This concept is a Truism – as this is the condition that is realized at Zero Point. However, the concept being discussed here is not about "duality" consciousness versus "unity" consciousness. The challenges or negative experiences on this plane of existence provide us with the opportunity to see things from the perspective of God. So, when observing something in our life or the life of another, that is clearly an adverse situation, we can choose how we will react to it. Do we find that we can become objective and not take it personally, or do we become judgmental or become angered by it? It provides us with the opportunity to turn the situation into one that we Master as opposed to having it mastering us.

Let's return to Newton for a moment. Some of our choice-re-actions are either positive or negative, and each one will serve as a force or catalyst to speed up our pace towards Self-Mastery or slow it down. But without the negative experience, we wouldn't have to make any choice at all. We would be living in harmony and peace for eternity, with nothing to propel us to our next spiritual level. Although you may not remember, you've made the decision to incarnate in a dense world so the unbalanced forces can help move you to the next phase of your spiritual journey.

The value of the Negative Polarity is essential for all of us. For those who have already attained a certain level of Spiritual Mastery, please try to understand that you need to be challenged here so that you can go to your next and highest level. Otherwise, you will experience stagnation. Remember that everything in Creation spirals upward to go Home to Zero Point or the Bosom of Creator. Just because one "Ascends" to a Higher Consciousness or reaches a Higher-Dimensional, or Higher-Vibratory Realm doesn't mean this is the end-all or end of the journey. The journey continues for all of Creation, perpetually and eternally. Even upon reaching Zero Point, there will be other quests and experiences – I am quite sure – as nothing in Creation is stagnant, but forever evolving and expanding. Even those that serve the Negative (Dark) Forces are in motion – slow motion, but in motion nonetheless.

SPIRITUAL AMNESIA

The caveat with "descending" into a world such as this is the amnesia. You experience severe amnesia about this process. Thank goodness that some of us can tap into our Soul Memory, which gives us an inkling into who we are and "Whom" we serve. The amnesia is put into place whenever we enter these lower worlds.

Why do you experience this "amnesia"? There are two very significant reasons that I will address here. The first cause for this amnesia is due to what is known as "being veiled" or The Veil. What does this word mean? According to the Merriam-Webster Dictionary, the word veiled is defined as: "a concealing curtain or cover of cloth or something that resembles a veil <a veil of stars>; especially: something that hides or obscures like a veil <lift the veil of secrecy>." For our purposes here, the word veiled means that a truth or truths are obscured or concealed from you. It is also an energetic cover that is placed over you before you take embodiment to hide your true origins and identity.

You come into this world "veiled" for very specific reasons. One reason is that you cannot function as a "native" of this world if you remember where you originally came from. It is enough of a shock to take embodiment in such a dense world, to experience all the limitations and challenges that come with being human. Some of these are the ailments and deterioration of the physical body; the suffering caused us by those of lower consciousness; and the drama created by our relationships with others. These challenges create stress and coping difficulties that affect your mind, your emotions, and your physical body. Life in this density is quite difficult for many. Now imagine how much harder it would be if you could remember what it is like to be in in those Realms of Bliss. You would probably be very depressed – maybe even suicidal.

A THIN VEIL

Some of us who have chosen to embody into physicality come in with thinner veils and, therefore, do remember our experiences in these Higher-Vibratory Realms. This memory or fragment of memory creates a less than favorable experience for us – one of resentment, disdain, loneliness, melancholy, reclusion, despair, suffering and jadedness.

I am one who experienced this. It was extremely difficult for me to accept that I was in the body of a young child, with certain unearthly powers, and a connection to a realm that was radiating light, beauty, and harmony. The realization of where I currently was and my physical limitations made me withdrawn and depressed. This "Knowing" and "longing" affected my childhood and early teens. My quest to find out who I was and why I felt different led me to seek God in a very profound way. It molded me into who I am today. Later in life, when memories of gatherings at the Higher Councils of Light returned, I realized that my being partially veiled was necessary and the plan for my life-stream all along. I had to know who I was from the get-go. I couldn't be the typical kid, having an ordinary childhood and teenage experiences because I would have gone down an entirely different path.

But there are some of you that remember "Home" and are truly miserable here. You wonder every day when this is going to be over. You have gotten bitter, suspicious, irritable, skeptical, intolerant and negative. Instead of using the knowledge, wisdom and the Light you carry within you to aide others and create a positive outcome, you use it to complain and sometimes curse your situation.

Not understanding the gift that is your life, the opportunity for exponential spiritual growth that comes with each difficult and negative challenge you face, you decide to be miserable and withdrawn. This mindset may be the reason that you see the glass as half empty, instead of half full. The glass that is filled halfway is just a glass that is filled halfway. Your perception of it is everything – and you'll base a whole philosophy on it and justify your negative behavior because you're "cursed" to only have half. The negative disposition that develops as a consequence is why being veiled is so imperative. It helps to prevent the pain that emanates in the soul when faced with the mechanics of this world. This pain will eat at you, sometimes preventing you from being fully engaged in your soul-mission and or achieving your Mastery.

The second reason for the amnesia or veiling is to provide a level playing field for your spiritual journey. What's the point of going on a scavenger hunt when you already know where the treasure is? The searching is part of the adventure. Your ability to discover the clues that eventually lead you to the treasure is what makes the whole thing worthwhile. The same is true of your spiritual journey – the thrill of discovery is the joy of the journey!

If you arrived here knowing all the answers, the nuances and the "ins and outs" of this labyrinth we call life, there would be no challenges and no opportunity to make choices that will lead to the discovery of how to get back Home. One of the reasons that Emissaries of Light, like us, choose to embody is to find our way back Home. We do so despite the fact that we don't remember how to get back and need to figure it out all over again. The task is to come in, while wearing the "spiritual blindfold", blending in with the "natives" of a world, and still make the same "correct" choices that lead us Home. Facing the challenges and making the right decisions every time is an enormous undertaking, and we are spiritual-masochists, doing it again and again and again. The obstacle is remembering who we are and staying focused, while interacting in a world that tempts us with worldly things and makes us forget that we are Sparks of The Divine.

Choosing correctly, embodiment after embodiment, demonstrates our Will and discipline to get back to God's Bosom. With this tenacity, we have little chance of being dissuaded or held back by the temptations provided in lower-density, Earth experiences. If we catch ourselves performing lower-density activities or behaviors, we should be able to recognize this and make the appropriate correction to stay on course – on the path of Illumination.

CHAPTER 4

THE COMPROMISED QUEST

"All warfare is based on deception. Hence, when we are able to attack,
we must seem unable; when using our forces, we must appear inactive;
when we are near, we must make the enemy believe we are far away;
when far away, we must make him believe we are near."

—Sun Tzu, "The Art of War"

If you originate from those Higher Realms, you probably were born here with a predisposition toward spirituality. Most of you have probably picked up a Bible or other sacred text at some point in your life, and began to inquire about Creation, and your purpose in it, at a relatively young age. Depending on what values your parents have given you, your focus could be on staying alive, being healthy, finding the right mate, leading an honorable life, and maybe having a good job. Maybe the focus was on working hard and saving up for retirement or being successful in business and acquiring wealth. So, you may start off with the predisposition for spirituality, but your external circumstances will take you down a more mundane path. And perhaps this is where your spiritual quest ends, as you're caught in the proverbial Hamster Wheel.

But for some of you, the search begins after realizing that going after mundane things doesn't fulfill you. You want to know the meaning and purpose of your life and why you're here now. If you fall in that group, you may know beyond a shadow of a doubt that you are here to do more than just get a big house or a high paying job. I am not saying there's anything wrong with these goals, only that you may be seeking spiritual comfort more than the comfort found in this world. For those with this objective, the aim then is to get closer to God, and to those Realms that are in your soul memory. You instinctively know that the answers to the perplexity of life and how to return to that Sacred Realm may be revealed by becoming more spiritual.

You may have begun the quest by going to the obvious place: traditional religion. After searching diligently there, you may find that information dispensed by religious institutions falls short – very short. It is laced with mistruths that are then used as a license to separate and to judge Prime Creator's Creation. If you follow the doctrine, according to its interpretation, then you're considered "good"; if you deviate from it in any way, you are considered "bad". Something doesn't sit right inside of you with respect to "The Doctrine". In other words, the doctrine conflicts with the inner "Knowing" of the "Truth" in your soul memory.

In your fervor to get to the Truth, you run into another body of information that explains why these doctrines have been misleading and why you have come out empty-handed. It seems the religion you had embraced omitted a lot of relevant information from its texts, and what was permitted to stay in and be called "sacred" contained a lot of misleading and infiltrated material. This discovery makes you mad and starts you off on another quest – one that will take up most of your waking hours in order to get to the "Real Truth".

You begin to acquire a new, deeper understanding of the making of the Universe and God. You realize that God is Prime or Supreme Creator – the Source of All That Is. You begin to see that everything comes from the Supreme and that we all have that Spark of The Divine within us. So in a nutshell, we are all God-Particles. This concept is a total contrast from the formalized religious point of view, where God is outside of us sitting on a throne. He needs to be pleased, is wrathful and jealous, and on top of that, we are dependent on others to connect to Him! And you wonder how this is so – why this (dis)information is being disseminated and why millions – billions – of people are following it.

When you start investigating this deeper, you find out that a great way to control the early populations on the planet was through fear. One way to program fear, as a constant, was to embed it in the culture of those to be governed so that it was self-generating. The result was the creation of religion. What is religion? According to Merriam-Webster Dictionary, it is defined as: "a set of beliefs concerning the cause, nature, and purpose of the universe, especially when considered as the creation of a superhuman agency or agencies, usually involving devotional and ritual observances, and often containing a moral code governing the conduct of human affairs."

So, after observing the inconsistencies that are taught in traditional religion; seeing how the masses are drawn to it and controlled by it; and then comparing our observation with the definition of what religion means, we need to ask who or what would put this in place and for what purpose? Something tampered with this information because there are too many examples of flawed thinking – words on a page that clearly do not depict the teachings found in The Illumined Realms of Prime Creator.

For example, if you were walking in a beautiful field, full of beautiful, colorful flowers that emit magnificent fragrances, and all of a sudden you encounter a solid, black flower whose aroma is just as pleasant as any flower before you, you wouldn't think, "Oh my...! God made a mistake with this one! What was He/She thinking? Let's pluck it. It doesn't belong here." I'm pretty sure you wouldn't think this at all. If you have a Higher Consciousness, you would probably determine that this is a unique flower, another magnificent creation and one that God decided to make stand out. Traditional religions, on the other hand, tend to criticize when someone does not mold to the misinterpreted, misdirected, misunderstood, misperceived, intentionally manipulated information that is presented in certain sacred texts.

I think you will agree that Creation – All Creation – is created by a Masterful Designer and Architect that is nameless, shapeless, genderless, beginningless and endless. This Supreme Creator has the ultimate intelligence to not make mistakes. The intention, orchestration and implementation of Its Creation are very precise and flawless. So, I will rephrase this: All of Creation has been "intended", conceived and birthed by a Prime/Supreme Creator without any mistakes. What I am stating here refers to the Original, Divine Blueprint or Design, and all expressions of this Creator in any given world and any given realm or universe. We are the ones, in this lower consciousness, that qualify Creator's Creation or define what is and isn't Its intention. We don't understand, perhaps, that Prime Creator expresses Itself through a Divine Palette, which allows for poetic license to bring diversity within Its Creations.

So, for example, to say that a gay man or woman is an aberration of nature – an abomination of God – belittles and second-guesses that God. Also, those who think that anyone, who according to the Bible and other Religious Texts is an abomination because they are of a different faith is also criticizing the Perfect God they worship. How can a God that is perfect and loving make something imperfect and/or hate it – especially when that God supposedly created everything and loves unconditionally?

THE CONUNDRUM

As many awaken to the inconsistencies, inaccuracies and disinformation provided by formalized religions, and the point of disgust sets in, an earnest quest for truth and a deeper connection with God begins. You may initiate the questioning process and have a lot of internal dialogs – sometimes with God. You may even find yourself in a mystical or metaphysical bookstore one day, picking up a copy of "The Celestine Prophecy", "Out on a Limb", "Many Lives, Many Masters", or other works. The information contained in these books starts you off on a journey of no return and opens up the floodgates that can never be closed again.

Books lead you to other books that reveal secrets that were hidden from you all this time. When you read the words on the page, they resonate in your heart. The words sing to you; they vibrate and are alive with what you deem to be Truth. The process of this discovery is very exciting. Many times you cry tears of gratitude for having found this information – again. You feel you're finally putting together the pieces of the puzzle, formulating a crystal clear picture that allows you to make sense of life experiences that have been less than kind. You come to the realization that these new concepts provide a freedom and connection to God that you've never experienced before. You begin to uncover groups and teachers that will help you go deeper into this knowledge and expand your awareness.

You then begin to attend workshops and lectures; you buy the CDs, DVDs, the books and workbooks. And shortly afterward, you discover that there are a myriad websites with information and free videos about all sorts of spiritual concepts. You begin to fill your mind and your time by joining different sites and engaging in online chats and blogs. And even though you have found an affinity with a group of people that are seekers just like you, you begin to notice that there are different ways of looking at the same thing.

You discover that various members of the "spiritual community" – the collective name for this group of spiritual seekers – view the Creation, God, the history of humanity and other such topics in a different way than you. But you gravitate more towards the information that originally sung to your heart, because it was so universal in scope. The concepts provided you with certain spiritual understandings that you didn't have before and gave your life meaning. You found a renewed purpose. You realize that what makes your heart sing is that which talks about Love and Light and Acceptance and Unity. You firmly recognize this to be the right path, because it resonates in your core as being Truth. You embrace the notion that "we are Gods" and "we create our reality" – two concepts that may have enthralled you because they make so much sense. Formalized religion kept this information away from you, and everyone else, since it would mean that humanity was divine and free and would no longer be under a control system. With this realization, you jumped out of the boiling pot known as religion and into another boiling pot – the New Age Movement.

As you begin to immerse yourself in this movement, you find that spiritual teachers and leaders were being diligently sought out for their information, information that was supposedly granted to them because of their spiritual attainment. They were the ones "in the know" and the ones allegedly receiving direct information from higher dimensions. Many of these new "household names" became known by channeling information given by so-called "Ascended Masters", "Archangels", "Jesus", ET Commanders, High Galactic Councils, etc. These teachers, leaders, gurus, and channelers were passing on information that contained Truisms that resonated with your soul memory.

Those hungry for new spiritual knowledge were turning to these so-called "enlightened" teachers and leaders for guidance;

however, many of these were not walking their talk. They were being "inspired" with disinformation, which in turn they would disseminate to their eager – and sometimes desperate – students. The students, who didn't know any better and happy to be in the flow of what they thought was higher-knowledge, embraced the concepts being presented, and a whole new mindset and beliefs were incubated in them.

This life-changing way of looking at The Universe, at Creation and ourselves was the key to understanding all of life's struggles. It was also "the ticket" out of a third-dimensional density and the entrance into a Fifth-Dimensional Earth. The assimilation of these new spiritual concepts meant no more suffering, no more illnesses or sadness – no more death. It was our admittance into what everyone knows as the Kingdom of Heaven, or "The New Earth."

So if these new concepts were supposed to empower us and help us in our journey out of this density, why are so many of us still ill? If these newly acquired understandings allowed us to be in tune with God – who is abundance – why are we still struggling financially? If this movement is about unconditional love and unity, then why are so many of us still lacking love, or are in separation – attacking one another? Why are we experiencing so much discord and so many failed relationships? Why do so many of us have so much drama and debilitating circumstances that are a constant factor in our lives? In short, why aren't our lives working?

CHAPTER 5

IT ISN'T WORKING!

"There are as many pillows of illusion as flakes in a snow-storm.
We wake from one dream into another dream."

—Ralph Waldo Emerson

After going through the motions of learning the lingo of this newly-acquired, spiritual path and participating in particular groups that reinforce these new perspectives, you may have realized that you feel great when interacting in that ambiance. But the great feeling isn't long-lasting. You feel "connected" to Mother Earth, the Moon, the Sun, the Cosmos – to everyone, everything and yourself when you're in the setting of the new spiritual path. You feel positive, in harmony, in a state of love, and you recognize the divinity in everything. And then, you go home, back to the situation(s) in your personal environment, and you face a disheartening truth: your life (still) isn't working for you. In fact, your life – as perceived by you – is trite, stagnant, inconsequential, meaningless, lonely, laborious and painful on many different levels.

If you're honest with yourself, you will realize that speaking the "spiritual talk" and reading all the books, buying the DVDs and attending the lectures isn't changing what's actually happening in your life. You try to paint a different picture of your reality when you're with others, especially those in the spiritual gatherings. Or you share what is happening in your life, but no matter what positive advice is given, nothing seems to work in correcting it. Sometimes after being given "good advice", you make light of the situation, too embarrassed to reveal that nothing has worked thus far.

It is a bit odd that in spite of the new spiritual infusion into your life, you sense that no progress is being made. You may be full of fear, have major hang-ups and weird pet peeves. You can't seem to overcome your stumbling blocks – some self-imposed, of course – that lead to an unfulfilled life. Overall, your life is very disappointing.

How is it possible that, supposedly, you've found "the code" that unlocks life's mysteries, expands your consciousness, and reveals the secrets of the ages, yet are still having negative experiences and dealing with unpleasant issues? Why is it that you're still in ill health, in bad moods, having self-esteem issues, in lack-mentality or feeling victimized? Why is it that you're still experiencing drama, stress, disintegrating relationships and financial problems? The inconsistency with what you're learning in the new spiritual path and what is currently being experienced is the conundrum most of us are faced with – no matter what religious faith we embrace or what spiritual path we follow.

You'll go to church on Sunday, feel great and empowered, go home and face reality: the bills are unpaid, the car isn't working, the plumbing is leaking, the air conditioner is broken, the kids are screaming, the in-laws are coming over and you can't stand them. Or, you'll attend an amazing meditation and ceremony, or a lecture with a much respected spiritual teacher, and then return home to find yourself in an altercation with someone, have to take your migraine medication or have to figure out if you have enough money in the bank to go grocery shopping.

You may have to deal with spouses that don't understand you or respect you, or family members who think you've gone off the deep end. And if you just happen to experience any paranormal or off-world experiences, you need to keep these to yourself because you don't want to be whisked away in a straitjacket. You become a loner, reclusive, strange and sometimes even delusional. To sum it up, this is not what you bargained for when you embodied here, and you resent the "bait and switch" and the fine, microscopic print on the enticing "Earth-Bound Brochure". You feel like a sucker.

You could also think that you're not being spiritual enough. So perhaps you get more crystals, do more Hail Marys, attend more Bible Studies, meditate more, go to more ceremonies with Native American Elders, or listen to "insightful" channeled messages. You are adamant about "cracking the code" to being happy right here and right now. You desperately want to free yourself from a life of strife, a life of grief, a life that you don't enjoy.

If it serves as some comfort, you are not alone. In fact, there are many people who are trying to get closer to God or are seeking spiritual experiences, yet are having issues with:

• Finances	• Anger
• Physical Health	• Fulfillment/Contentment
• Mental Health	• Self-Esteem
• Emotional Health	• Self-Realization/Self-Actualization
• Addictions	• Self-Reliance
• Relationships	• Taking Action
• Family	• Joy
• Trust	• A Disconnection from Source-Creator

So why has this happened? One reason is that some of us don't take responsibility for our actions, our thoughts or emotions; we go outside ourselves for answers, guidance and for quick-fixes to the problems we face. The spiritual path you follow is only as good as how you choose to use it, and your willingness to apply what you've learned. It should serve as a stepping stone for the Higher Understandings that lead to Truth – with a capital T. Everything else provided here, in this third-dimensional-reality, is prone to mis-interpretation, to deceit and as a means of control. Any spiritual "truth" that comes from this Lower-Vibrational Realm is more than likely mixed with misleading, erroneous, deceitful and manipulated information, created for the purpose of:

+ Making you dependent on others for the "truth" – since you may feel you're not spiritually mature enough to do it on your own.

+ Keeping you in the dark – so that you don't receive all the information or accurate information.

+ Having you chase the "Spiritual Carrot" – which, in this case, would be the Rapture, the Ascension, a Transformation or a Shift of Consciousness, or a Fifth-Dimensional Earth.

+ Trapping you in this reality or Matrix – that isn't pleas-ant and serves as a way to cause grief and other negative emotions.

You are probably experiencing the negative aspects of your personal reality and in a very pronounced way. The moments of positive experiences are far and few in between and are illusive. The negative experiences are more recurring and magnified. Because these make such a profound impression in your psyche, you tend to become angry and bitter at your situation, which then serves to attract more negative experiences.

Then, you become jaded and even worse – resentful. You formulate an opinion that everything you've learned up to now from your religious practice or new spiritual path seems to be working for everyone else but you. You then conclude that 1) You're not worthy and are "spiritually challenged", or 2) No one, not even the spiritual leaders or teachers are impervious to what you're going through and that behind closed doors, everyone is experiencing their own form of "hell". If conclusion number two is correct, who will confess this? No one will because this will invalidate the spiritual teaching they are standing behind.

What you are witnessing here is a "spiritual miasma", an illness or virus that has been surgically inserted into the spiritual framework – for all spiritual paths. Because you want to know your roots, and find your way back Home, or connect to something higher than yourself, with the hope of finding relief from the pain of existence, you are more prone to sabotage via the "spiritual arena". This is the venue of choice used to keep you docile and placated by providing you with the answer to most of your questions; you are given just enough to meet your needs and to keep you longing for that familiar resonance from your "True Home".

You're given the hope that you'll return "Home" at some point in *this* embodiment, so you continue getting up in the morning. You're given the props and the "set" – like a theater – to make you believe you're on the path to God. All along you're really like a goldfish in an aquarium who thinks that the gravel, the plants, and the decorations are its original home – it doesn't know it's in a fake environment.

You become complacent by the lulling words of "truth", words that feel warm, and reassuring. Along with that, you also have a false belief that you've got the ticket to Nirvana with these newly discovered secrets. So you take the posture that there's nothing left for you to do but wait, and the suffering will soon stop – because we're all so close to "The Return". It's a deliberately engineered mechanism to keep you thinking you're a step or two away from third-dimensional freedom, when all along the program is meant to keep you in the cage one year after the next. It keeps you hanging on to the hope of this imaginary freedom, year after year, decade after decade, century after century, millennium after millennium. You wait and wait, and nothing happens – because nothing will. Yet, you're made to believe that something magical will occur to break you, and humanity, from bondage. In the meantime, you suffer and you hang on.

Who or what would design such a devious and sadistic program? Only something with off-world, incredible intelligence and power would be able to design, engineer and orchestrate such a plan. The architects of this are known as The Opponent, The Dark Forces, The Sinister Forces or The Negative Forces. Everything else, which is negative or of an evil nature, is in service to The Opponent. These Forces are real. It's a part of this world and reality, and it's interfering with everyone's life and our liberation from this very challenging Earth experience. The quicker you understand what this is, the quicker you'll get your life working the way it was intended by Prime Creator.

"Thus we may know that there are five essentials for victory:

1. He will win who knows when to fight and when not to fight.

2. He will win who knows how to handle both superior and inferior forces.

3. He will win whose army is animated by the same spirit throughout all its ranks.

4. He will win who, prepared himself, waits to take the enemy unprepared.

5. He will win who has military capacity and is not interfered with by the sovereign."

—Sun Tzu, "The Art of War"

PART II
KNOWING THE OPPONENT

CHAPTER 6

A FORCE GONE AWRY

"For our struggle is not against flesh and blood, but against the rulers, against the authorities, against the powers of this dark world and against the spiritual forces of evil in the heavenly realms."

—**Ephesians 6:12**

The subject matter presented in this section is heavy and may be difficult to get through. You may also find that you become a bit sleepy because the left brain has a hard time comprehending many of the concepts. There will be a very sharp contrast to how the previous chapters have made you feel up to now and how you will feel after reading this material. But, as unpleasant as it is, this part of our reality needs to be addressed, and looked at with courage and great resolve, as it forms most of what all of us experience in this world, and is in direct opposition to the Will and Original Blueprint of Prime Creator.

Part of your skill-set for Mastery on this plane is being razor-sharp and vigilant, aware and discerning, courageous and proactive. While many who have a Muslim or Judeo-Christian background are familiar with the concept of Satanic Forces and Lucifer, many in the spiritual community do not give credence to an "Opponent", or Force that acts in direct opposition to The Light that we represent. Maybe it is a subject matter that elicits fear in some of us or is part of the new spiritual indoctrination that we currently embrace. Many ask how there can be an Opponent when everything is one? That's a great question, and it has a great answer – that will be discussed later on. Unfortunately many of the Truisms of modern-day spirituality are too broad and too generalized, making the framework for all the information provided by these to be extremely loose – it's a "one size fits all". A concept is found to be true, as it resonates in everyone's core, yet what is truly behind that truth is left out. Therefore the understanding of when this applies is not revealed – much like the teachings of Jesus or the Higher Teachings from other Masters and sacred texts, where the true meaning of the concepts are lost, or misinterpreted. We can also call this "selective spirituality" – where we choose what the interpretation of the information is based on our beliefs, life experiences or our perception-filters.

Much of Jesus' teachings were more than likely removed from the New Testament. Do we still think that the red lettering, representing Jesus' words in the New Testament, is the only thing Jesus said or taught the entire time he was teaching? Surely there was much more intricate and in-depth knowledge that was disseminated all that time He was amongst His followers. Where is it? All you hear about are the same specific stories and quotes recorded by four different apostles that could have covered more of what Jesus taught. Instead, they pretty much jotted down different versions of the same events. How is this possible?

Sometimes, in order to get to the real Truth of a more simplistic truth – the one-size-fits-all type – you need to dig a bit deeper, and let go of the mind altogether. By shutting down the mind and going within your heart, which is the home for your Knowing, you will KNOW the Truth. The heart is your connection to Source

Creator and your access to Eternal Wisdom and Eternal Truth. So, let's start exercising the Knowing Muscle now. Connecting to that Higher Wisdom helps you to navigate through all the marketing and propaganda given to you not only from Madison Avenue, but from pseudo, spiritual teachings that present you with concepts and understandings that are untruths. And the connection to the Higher Wisdom of Prime Creator is our Discernment – with a capital "D."

VIBRATION

The Opponent is not a particular person or an entity, but a Force. Many people mistake the Opponent with the Devil, Satan, Lucifer, archons, and demons. What is being discussed here is that Force that is in direct opposition to The Light that represents the Positive Polarity of Prime Creator. The Opponent is the Negative Polarity and all the aspects and attributes of that. It is that Force that governs and animates those that serve it: the Devil, Satan, Lucifer, archons, demons, djinn, negative discarnate beings, negative ET Races and the earth-based minions and cohorts in human form. Its original purpose was to create a balance, as it sits on the opposite side of the Light spectrum. Each side of this "balance" is also referred to as "polarity". The Light represents the Positive Polarity, and the Dark represents the Negative Polarity. Darkness, as is used here, does not mean a color or lack of light, but a vibration. Vibration makes up this Universe and everything in this Creation. Each manifestation in Creation carries its own vibratory signature of energy frequency that makes it what it is.

The Light is of the ultimate, finest, most sublime and highest vibration. In the Higher Realms, the electrons move so rapidly, that these Realms and Beings residing in them cannot be seen with our physical eyes. One of the reasons is that our physical eyes are currently in a physical body that is of a third-dimensional density. In this density or dimension, our electrons move slower.

As I mentioned earlier, Prime Creator at rest is Every "thing" and No "thing" in particular. It contains everything in Its Creation. Included in this description are all manifestations of the myriads of emanations and expression-potentials to be birthed utilizing the Divine Blueprint, which have the freedom to elect their life-stream path. Therefore, It is the Light and the Dark, Positive and Negative, Male and Female, Blessed and Cursed, White and Black and all the colors in between. It is The All That Is. In this state of "Isness", Prime Creator is at the Highest-Vibrational Frequency.

As I've mentioned previously, in order to create various Realms, Creator lowers Its vibration, stepping it down more and more by compressing The Light, creating the Lower Realms with every compression. It continues the "stepping down process" until It reaches our level of density. At this third-dimensional level, the electrons' "dance" has been slowed down so much that it's almost at a standstill – when compared to that of the Illumined Realms. The slowing down of the vibration or movement of electrons creates Physicality and dense matter.

Imagine water, liquid H2O, in a boiling tea kettle. At some point, the particles of the water are so agitated, because of the increasing heat, that they start moving further apart until it changes from being in a liquid state to a vapor. The electrons are so loose or separated that it's hard to see the new form or expression of the H2O. But as it hits the cooler air, it creates what looks like clouds or steam. And if you hold a plate directly over the steam, you will notice the formation of water droplets. The droplets occur due to the cooler temperature slowing down the electrons so that it turns back into liquid form. If you freeze this, the cold temperature will cause a further slowdown of these electrons to form solid ice.

FREQUENCY MATCH

Your third-dimensional eyes cannot see the Higher-Vibrational Realms or Beings who dwell there because there is no frequency match – normally. It is similar to sitting down on your couch at home when it is a hot summer day, and you put on the ceiling fan. First you put it on low. You look up and see the brown blades rotating slowly. Let's say you notice one of the blades is much lighter in color so that it's noticeable. You follow this one blade with your eyes, watching it as it spins slowly. Now, you increase the speed of the fan. The blades begin to move a bit faster and faster. You now have a hard time distinguishing the lighter-colored blade from the rest. And as you increase the speed, the blades appear to blend, forming a blur of the spinning blades – similar to the propeller of a plane.

When you put the fan at maximum speed, something interesting happens. Let's say you sit down on the couch and look to catch a glimpse of that lighter-colored blade. You won't be able to see it anymore. The fan is going so fast that all you can see is the ceiling – you see right through the blades! The blades seem to have become invisible. How is this possible? It's due to the speed that the blades are rotating. The fan is going so fast that it seems as if the blades aren't there anymore. It gives the impression that they are coming in and out of this reality. You would be like a third-dimensional observer trying to see an object that is in another frequency or dimension. If you were able to jump on the blades, then you would be traveling at the same speed, and you would be able to see them again.

By the same token, if you are a third-dimensional being, with electrons that are slowed down so that you can express in this world of matter, you will not be able to see a High-Vibrational Being, whose electronic speed is much faster. You would have to raise your vibration high enough to match the vibration of that Being – or the Being would have to lower its vibration.

LOWER-VIBRATORY STATES

The opposite of this High-Vibratory state is the low-vibratory state or Low-Vibratory Realms. Because the Light of Creator has been compressed and compressed, stepping down the Luminosity and electron movement with each Realm that moves away from the point of origin or Zero Point, the Realms become denser and denser, until most of the Light is obscured or veiled. This opaqueness is what is known as "The Lesser Light". In this case, the electronic movement is slow; therefore, the vibration is low. In Low-Vibratory Realms, we experience density, gravity, space, time, and matter.

In these Lower-Vibratory Realms, "beings" that are not in physicality – known as demons, negative discarnate beings and entities, and their masters – thrive. These Lower Realms are their home away from Home, as these originated from Source as well. The original purpose and plan for their expression or existence is to provide negative experiences for us in order to accomplish Self-Mastery. These lower-vibratory entities in service to self, collectively known as Dark Forces, provide an array of negative experiences in what we can call Earth-U. These experiences put us on the spot. We have to choose between living in strife and suffering, or desiring to be even more connected with that which is Perfection, Luminous, Joyful, and Balanced. The Positive states, if you can raise your vibration and consciousness enough to experience them, will allow for a life of ease and positive results. The choice has to be made, because if you don't choose how you will deal with your pain, suffering, drama and other unfavorable situations, the default is getting the same and more negative experiences. Attracting more negative circumstances will continue until you learn how to surpass these events in your life in equanimity, humility, and gratitude – and that is not an easy feat. There are not too many that will be thankful for the bad hand that life has dealt them or be neutral about it!

You may fail miserably at this – as most of us do. You may not have the spiritual fortitude or physical strength or vitality to muster up enough high vibration, using every ounce of a Higher Consciousness in its infancy to pull you through those very dark moments. With each failure, the idea that you can't overcome any ailments or difficulties in your life is reinforced. You come to believe the toxic soup of negative experiences as being part of your spiritual makeup and personal reality. As a consequence, you go into a "woe is me" mentality – a victim mentality. You know the general principals of spirituality, but you can't seem to put them into practice when it counts, and you begin to question if spirituality even works. Then you become angry at life, bitter, cynical, jaded, apathetic, miserable – states that further serve to lower your personal vibration. And, of course, the lower in vibration you go, the worse it gets and the harder it becomes to leave "The Matrix".

Not all adverse situations, though, are meant to provide life-transforming lessons that we can grow from to become stronger. These other experiences, pernicious ones, are meant to derail us physically, mentally, emotionally and spiritually. I will discuss this in the chapters that follow.

CHAPTER 7

TACTICS AND STRATEGY OF THE OPPONENT

"If your enemy is secure at all points, be prepared for him. If he is in superior strength, evade him. If your opponent is temperamental, seek to irritate him. Pretend to be weak, that he may grow arrogant. If he is taking his ease, give him no rest. If his forces are united, separate them. If sovereign and subject are in accord, put division between them. Attack him where he is unprepared, appear where you are not expected."

—Sun Tzu, "The Art of War"

Here's something that might be shocking to you, or maybe not, depending on how much of this stuff you've studied already. The Opponent *also* contains the thimbleful of the ingredients or attributes of Prime Creator. However, those that reside in these Lower-Vibratory Realms are masterminds and tenacious creators of havoc, not harmony or balance, as this is their path of choice. They are the total opposite of the Positive Polarity. They have a plan, and they're sticking to it – and *sticking it to us* in the process.

As I mentioned earlier, these Forces, which are in direct opposition to the Light Forces, create conditions that are meant to help you grow spiritually – when they're following the guidelines or protocols of Prime Creator. Of course, this is not the way the story goes in "real-time". In real-time, these Forces have gone rogue or have decided on a different path. They are completely in service-to-self and are running this planet, and many other planets, unfortunately. They are that proverbial bad strain that escaped the petri dish and is now going pandemic! Why this happened is the topic of another book; for now, we're concerned with the fact that it happened and that it's affecting everyone in this reality.

These nefarious ones have a mission, and that is to throw every curveball possible at you – not to help you grow spiritually but to stunt your spiritual growth. Therefore, they exist for the purpose of preventing you from achieving your highest spiritual attainment. This new directive is a sharp contrast to what their original mission was. The new modus operandi for these spiritual terrorists is to make sure none of us "Return Home"; they also aim to dethrone Prime Creator and put themselves in that seat, as if this were even possible. They're arrogant, and a bit delusional, certainly, but the fact is they do have a lot of power. I'll get into that in a bit; for now, suffice it to say that this power was given to them originally, but now they're running with it. They're making sure we all fail at achieving Mastery once again, and that Prime Creator doesn't experience the Return of *Its* Creation.

When I think of what they're doing, it reminds me of an Olympic marathon runner who is in first place and approaching the finish line when a fan of one of the other runners throws an icy, cold soft drink at him. It hits his face and splatters, shocking him. In just those few micro-seconds, he loses his footing and momentum while all the other runners are pushing themselves harder to cross the finish line first. Consequently, the stunned runner loses first place and the prize. It's cheating, it's dirty, it's poor form, and this is how the Dark Forces work. We cannot expect them to be ethical.

Here is a very important fact: the Opponent or Dark Forces do not play fair or by the same rules as the Positive-Polarity or Light Forces. They do not abide by the "Universal Code of Conduct" or Rules of Engagement of any of the Higher Councils of Light. They abide only by their rules, even when Protocols have been set in place about how to engage humanity and life on Earth. And because these Forces are no longer working in cooperation with The Divine Plan of Prime Creator, they govern themselves and create their own blueprints and agendas.

These Forces going rogue was not always the case. Originally, those serving the Dark Forces were commissioned by Creator to dwell in the lower-density worlds as part of *The Plan*. It was intentional. However, their lust to rule and enslave humanity and other races, thus preventing all of us from freeing ourselves from this realm, was not intentional or part of the Original Plan. Again, these Forces are masterminds. They are ruthless, clever, sly, conniving, work in stealth and are very deceptive. They have infiltrated everything on this planet and other worlds as well. On this planet, this includes the media, governments, religion and other institutions for the purpose of confusing, hypnotizing, dumbing-down, taming and controlling humanity.

If you're thinking this sounds like something straight out of a science fiction movie, you're right! But it's my belief that the writers of science fiction movies are taking their material directly from our reality. These Forces are no longer shy and secretive about what they're up to and have stepped up their game-plan. They're boastful about their blatant misdeeds and unprecedented evil-doings.

If you pay close attention to the escalating global events, you will notice a new kind of evil – that which is beyond barbaric and tramples on all life. This new type of morphed-malevolence is not something that is conceived in the minds of regular men or women.

It is incubated in the lair of that which has become an abomination – a grotesquerie. It is a miscreation or a creation of something that is purposefully in direct opposition to what it was supposed to be.

Clearly, this is not part of the Original Plan of Creator, as part of the Plan was to give Its Creation the freedom to select its path back to Itself. We cannot look the other way, pretending this does not exist. This malevolence is happening every day; it is a part of the world in which we are living, and we must be cognizant of and vigilant against it. Most importantly, we must realize that it is being generated and fueled by these Dark Forces.

Because you're currently a member of the human race, you cannot take a stance of apathy or indifference, especially if you serve The Light and Prime Creator. This world is out of balance, and it affects all sentient beings and all life-forms. It is our responsibility, as the representatives of The Light in embodiment, to help raise the consciousness and vibration of humanity. Whenever possible, we should alert people to what is happening "behind the scenes" worldwide, especially because they've been too busy to notice or care. And we should also present them with tools that will give them the opportunity to raise their own consciousness and vibration so that they too can ward off attacks by these Forces.

The concept is simple. Imagine you're observing a little child playing innocently in the garden, and you notice a poisonous snake slithering towards him. Do you look away as the snake attacks? Do you shrug your shoulders and say, "Oh, well…"? Do you pretend the snake isn't there? Of course not. As a representative of the Illumined Worlds, you do not have this luxury; you are here to serve humanity. To be aware of what is happening on the planet and shrug it away is not only irresponsible but has repercussions for everyone who chooses this attitude and behavior. The choice to do nothing creates a ripe environment for malevolence to thrive! So, helping to create awareness, taking action and leading by example are some of the things we all should be doing unceasingly.

Needless to say, this is no easy task. In fact, you may already be tired of trying to create awareness by blogging, talking and sharing information, only to be met with resistance and animosity. It won't be easy to create this awareness, especially when so many have been desensitized and hypnotized by the media and other marketing strategies. I get less resistance from what is known as the "unaware masses" than from the so-called "enlightened" community. My observation is that many of the unaware genuinely want to know; whereas most of the "pseudo-enlightened" think they've already reached the apex of knowledge.

Still, we cannot give up – the Opponent doesn't! These Dark Forces do not get tired or worn out. They don't say: "Guess it's time to go home" or "It's not my responsibility" or "It's not my fight." These representatives of the Dark Forces are resilient, tenacious, consistent, adamant, persistent and voracious. They're at it twenty-four-seven – non-stop, and we must be as well; otherwise we might as well raise the white flag now. And although many of the so-called spiritual community feel that they should send them love and light, it is important to understand that these creatures or "miscreations" do not respond to this. This type of Higher Consciousness and Higher-Vibratory response is not accepted or recognized by them.

The good news is that by maintaining awareness and being vigilant and proactive, you have the opportunity for amazing spiritual strength and growth. You also get to add your Light, your talents and expertise to the pot, so that you can help turn things around. As you become proactive in bringing awareness to the planet, you help empower others, and by empowering others, you also grow spiritually. It is the chance of a lifetime and one of the big reasons you're here. The Dark Forces are escalating their tactics and refining their game-plan. What are you going to do about it? Do you refrain from participation and continue to live your life as if everything will magically fix itself one day, or do you decide to come out of your shell and start contributing towards the solution? That choice is yours.

PERSONAL ATTACKS

You may be receiving incredible protection from the Host of Heaven. As a consequence, you may not be experiencing many, or any, personal attacks from the Dark Forces and those who serve it. The reason is because you've probably connected with the Higher-Vibratory Realms and have made direct contact with those Beings of Light, also known as The Host of Heaven. The Host of Heaven – the Light Forces – serves Prime Creator and all Its Creation. One of their tasks is to guard and protect those that summon their help, especially those who also serve The Light. But in order for them to intervene on your behalf, you need to have established direct communication with Source-Prime Creator so that your vibration is of the highest octave possible.

It is difficult for these Lower-Vibratory Forces to mess with someone who has raised their vibration and continuously stays in communication with The Higher Realms and Prime Creator. What happens is that there is a battle that transpires in the Astral Realm between the Light Forces and the Dark Forces. The end-result is usually not in favor of the Dark Forces, but they try regardless because they're just waiting for the opportunity to get you into a lowered vibration. When they get you to display negative emotions, you provide them with all the motivation they need to keep trying. For them, this is like a free, "all-you-can-eat" feast at a buffet. They feed on your emotions of doubt, grief, fear, despair, anguish, hopelessness and more.

Again, these Forces fabricate a situation in your life that makes you react with one of the many negative emotions you have at your disposal. Often, you don't even realize you have a choice – your emotions take over, and you just act out. An inappropriate reaction lowers your vibration. Once it's lowered, they introduce another situation that makes you respond in a negative fashion, which lowers your vibration even more.

There is a sinister agenda with this vicious cycle. Each time a new situation is introduced it becomes graver than the one before it, and your reaction becomes more severe than the previous reactions. You become weaker and weaker, as each situation is worsened, and your reaction is aggravated by these experiences. It leaves you drained and in a state of despair so that you can't fight off the next episode. If you don't realize what is happening and how you are being milked for *loosh* or negative emotional energy, you will keep experiencing negative situations. These negative, astral creatures in service to the denser, dark lords or dark rulers will not stop at just one feeding. Having identified an easy prey, they will use your life-force to provide them with multiple feedings, usually throughout your lifetime. You have become energetic live-stock.

INTERPERSONAL ATTACKS

At some point in this earthly incarnation, you've probably experienced a rupture in your relationship with family members and friends, co-workers and professional or business associates that didn't make sense. One moment you were fine, laughing and enjoying each other's company, and the next you were mortal enemies. It made even less sense when whatever caused this rift was trivial or insignificant. It was perhaps significant to you and/or the other person at the time, but intrinsically – and from a much Higher Perspective – it was total minutia.

How does something so frivolous become so grave – and how does it escalate to the point of rupturing long-time friendships and relationships with family members? How does the communication at work or in a business scenario get so messed up that it affects your ability to function properly first at work and then at home? What causes you to perceive a situation in a manner that affects your judgment and results in a negative reaction? The answer is dark entities.

These entities, which thrive in low vibration, are responsible for most interpersonal relationship challenges. They are astral parasites that love to create scenarios and manipulate people's perceptions in order to elicit a particular response from their chosen target. Most of those unsuspecting targets have weaknesses in their emotional fortitude or their spiritual make-up, and these weaknesses, especially openings in their auric field, are their Achilles Heel. The prize for these entities is to compromise those that have spiritual awareness or have attained a certain spiritual level. To knock these Light Emissaries off their horse by discombobulating them emotionally is top-prize! An emotional tailspin lowers that person's vibration and the entities go into their feeding frenzy.

But it's not over after they feed. There is this prolonged and lingering resentment and hurt that remains even after the distressing situation is over. Think of what happens after you've had a fight with someone. Often, the stress does not end with the argument; instead, we replay the mental video of the ordeal over and again. Each time it brings back the negative emotions and provides the entities with another feast. For those with spiritual understanding, or who are on the planet to uphold the Light and work on uplifting the consciousness of humanity, this slows their momentum or even derails them altogether. Sometimes, it even completely paralyzes them, robbing them of their desire to continue on the path of The Light or serve others in any capacity. This condition helps to take down a Light Emissary or Spiritual, Light Warrior. When this happens to many

Light Emissaries, it creates a defeat for the Light Forces because it drains their strength and hinders their mission to help shift the consciousness of humanity and implement change.

The Opponent accomplishes this by individually picking out the members of the Light Forces and weakening the Light-Collective. The Dark Forces can't interfere with the Light Forces when we're united, so they find personal weaknesses or weaknesses in our auric field. They hone in on emotional fragility due to traumatic experiences. Then they aggravate a situation by skewing the perception of one or both of the parties involved in the altercation – especially if either is emotionally vulnerable. These Negative Forces are keen on knowing just where we are vulnerable and how to squeeze the maximum amount of negative-emotion-juice out of us.

It's complicated, yet simple at the same time. The Dark Forces are masters of illusion and trickery. They make it seem as if it's the other person that is the aggressor or culprit when all along it's the Dark Forces. They are probably targeting you because you have a tendency to misperceive and go into emotional meltdown. If you've had a traumatic experience and currently have self-esteem issues, for example, you may perceive your world very differently than someone who doesn't have these experiences or issues. You see the world through these lenses, have built up coping mechanisms to deal with perceived wrongs, and react accordingly. The Dark Forces then manipulate your perceptions accordingly, to fit your belief system.

Let say, for example, two coworkers are having a conversation. One says to the other, "You aren't doing this correctly...", and while they said it in a neutral tone, the other person, who has experienced trauma in the past, perceives them as being condescending, belittling and reprimanding. In fact, he is sure he is being called stupid, incapable, retarded, imperfect, and so on and so forth – all projections from his mind or what he feels he is.

The traumatized individual will then replay in his head an old tape of someone who belittled him during a vulnerable time in his life. He listens to the words being spoken to him now, and although these words carry no energetic, emotional charge or negativity with them, to him, they are the same. Then his ego steps in to further mess up the perception and tells him that this is the same scenario as before and that he's being verbally and emotionally abused.

This traumatic memory leads him to respond in a manner that is confrontational and defensive. And no matter what the other person says to the contrary, the mind is made up that this person is out to hurt him and humiliate him. Then the other person begins to get riled because the tone and attitude of the individual with the misperception is uncalled for, and there's a need to stop an unwarranted accusation. The next thing that transpires is a heated argument. It escalates to such a point that feelings are not only hurt, but deep scars are formed. Negative emotions – negative energy –spews out generously and bountifully, providing food for the Dark Forces, which include all the parasitic, low-vibratory expressions residing in the Astral Realm. All the voracious predators come out for the feed!

Now, if the two people involved in this confrontation just happen to be Light Emissaries, Light Warriors, Way Showers or Movers and Shakers in the Light Community, this could cause emotional fatigue on any of the parties involved. It could cause either party to lose their drive and want to discontinue their mission. It can create stagnation so that a project or task doesn't move forward. This lack of engagement gives the opportunity for the opposition to advance. This technique used by the Dark Forces is the famous Divide and Conquer method. They place adverse ideas in our heads. They also mess with our emotional bodies or use past trauma and insecurities to make us misjudge a situation and cause such animosity that it separates us – leaving us wide open and easy targets for further interference!

If this has happened to you in the past, you are not alone. But now that you know what causes these situations, you can deal with things differently in the future. Because of who you are "in Truth", because of the real reason you have embodied into this density, you have a serious responsibility to move out of ego and look at everything from a much Higher and objective perspective. If you don't, you think that the other person is at fault, when all along you are being played like a fiddle. You may even still be holding on to grudges many years after an altercation has taken place. In doing so, you give victory to the Opponent by lowering your vibration with every negative emotion you experience as you conjure up the memory. And by having these old tapes play in your head, allowing you to justify your bitterness and anger, you place yourself in "separation" so that the Light Forces don't unify or get stronger.

Your inability or undesirability to understand how these Forces work will keep you weak and in the "dark". Your inefficiency in recognizing the Opponent's strategies and how all of us are intentionally separated from one another so that we can be taken down is what is keeping this spiritual slaughter in place. Not observing the symptoms of an *interpersonal interaction* gone awry, not being sensitive to the dark energy created in an argument or all-out misunderstanding gives credit to the Opponent and speaks to how easily we – the Light Emissaries – are manipulated, toyed with, divided and conquered. If we were more astute in our perceptions and were willing to understand the enemy – what these are capable of doing and how they do it – then we would have the upper hand by making better emotional choices.

MENDING A RELATIONSHIP RUPTURE

Rising above situations that cause interpersonal ruptures happens when you tap into the Divine Self of the other person. But first, you need to tap into your own Divine Self so that you don't get suckered into the fabricated situation in front of you. Instead of getting agitated when you don't see eye-to-eye, when you perceive someone is wronging you or belittling you, it is wise to observe the energy and the patterning of the behavior and see if you can determine that it's not coming from your own Divinity or the other person's Divinity, but something less than that, something of lower vibration. And if this is the case, then it's the Opponent who is manipulating and orchestrating the situation.

The Light does not manipulate or orchestrate anything in order to hurt, separate, rupture, deceive, obscure, confuse, mislead, misperceive, or allow for misinterpretation. The Light is Transparent, Pure, True, Pristine, Clean, Direct, and Joyful. Thus, you must approach the confrontation with a clear understanding of what these Negative Forces are trying to accomplish. Then you must lift your consciousness so that you can see the situation from a much higher perspective, a perspective that gives clarity and objectivity.

We also need to come from a place of humility, putting ego aside, and approach the situation with a clear mind, with an open heart and a desire for Higher Understanding. This level of spiritual maturity happens when you tap into Prime Creator Energy – that energy at Zero Point where everything is Pristine and in Harmony and Unified according to the Original Blueprint of Creator-Intention.

Once you're aware of what is transpiring in a discordant interaction, it is up to you to try to mitigate it, diffuse it or walk away from it. If you are a Servant of the Light, one that serves Prime Creator, you cannot, having this "awareness", continue an argument or engage in discord. If you do, you are not raising your consciousness beyond the limitations of this density. You become like a puppet for the puppeteers – the Dark Forces/Controllers of this world – allowing them to do with you what they will. You need to exert more control over your thoughts and emotions and master these so that the Dark Forces don't become your masters.

It is optimal to behave in a Christ-like manner with one another. If you know that all low-vibratory emotions are triggered by Dark Forces, it will be in your best interest and the best interest of all involved in a dispute to come from a place of humility. This demeanor is an example of the reserved, self-confidence of a True

Master. Therefore, one of the greatest things you can do is extend a hand and forgive as well as ask for forgiveness for any hurt you may have caused. It is difficult to do at first and can be humiliating, especially if you haven't yet Mastered Ego.

Even if you weren't the instigator, even if you were not at fault, even if you were misinterpreted, or the situation misperceived, be the one to extend the hand in friendship. If you truly want to step into your Mastery, this is what a Master does. There is no emotional charge; there is only a state of love, peace, harmony and neutrality. You do this not so much for the other person in the altercation, but for your personal spiritual growth and attainment. If the other person sees this gesture and is transformed by it, then there are two souls that have overcome the challenge!

Just because you deem yourself spiritual or "enlightened" doesn't mean you are immune to these attacks or interference by the Dark Forces. As a matter of fact, they are very much attracted to your light. They're after the potential of a "quick fix" by provoking you and getting you to react to situations that are fabricated and/or manipulated by them. The more light you have, the more they are attracted to you. So, when you see a lot of hurdles in your life, challenges that you know are not normal and feel contrived; when you experience blatant interference, you can rest assured that you are one that carries a lot of light, and they want your light turned off by lowering your vibration.

CHRIST CONSCIOUSNESS VERSUS THE OPPONENT

According to the New Testament, Jesus was tempted three times by one of the Dark Lords, otherwise known as Satan or the Devil. This "Lord" was extremely clever and played to situations that would otherwise cause weakness. The first interference in trying to get Jesus to waver in his Mastery was when He was forty days without food. The Dark Lord tells Jesus to turn the stones into bread (Matthew 4:3-4). The second temptation occurs when this Dark Lord says to Him that if He is the Son of God, to throw Himself down from the pinnacle of the temple, that God would send His angels to catch Him. The Dark Lord was attempting to get Jesus to abuse His powers (Matthew 4:5-7). The third attempt, the Dark Lord asks Jesus for His allegiance, giving Him a quick path to the Messiahship, bypassing the crucifixion and passion and giving Him all the Kingdoms of the world and their glory (Mathew 4:8-10).

It takes a very advanced soul to see through the trickery, to be steadfast in its allegiance to The Light of Supreme Creator, to make the right choices and to act using Christ Consciousness. You may not be there yet. You may struggle every day just to put a smile on your face or to utter a kind word when a kind word is the last thing you want to say. In the middle of a major discord, it could take all of your might to remember who you are and who that other person is – A Divine Spark of Prime Creator. Regardless of how spiritually elevated you think you are, you more than likely have had your cage rattled by someone or some event, and the negative energy was so thick you could cut it with a knife.

I'm pretty sure you've heard the saying, "Fake it till you make it." If you act like a Christed Being and emulate what a Christed Being would do in each given situation, it may just rub off on you. You might end up with a super-evolved, elevated Christ Consciousness by the time it's all said and done! Practice makes perfect – so they say – and I know this is so. Practice what a Christed Being would do in a situation that would otherwise generate negative emotions and the opportunity to attain Self-Mastery and Christ Consciousness will be forthcoming.

They say it takes twenty-one days to form a new habit. Maybe it takes longer; but if you intend on acquiring this habit, who cares how long it takes? Just begin the process of being in this new state of Christ Consciousness. Practice it continuously for thirty days without fail. The change you will see in yourself may be the Consciousness Shift or Ascension that you've been seeking. The surprise is that this "graduation" to Higher Consciousness or Ascension has been in your hands all along.

Can you imagine the disappointment of the Dark Forces when they can no longer get you to lower your vibration, can no longer get you to lose your composure or take things personally? Yes, they'll get angry because there'll be no more feedings. And yes, they'll try even harder. That, unfortunately, is just the way it goes on this plane. However, if you Master your emotions, you're on your way to true sovereignty and liberation from this third density reality. But first you need to understand what else these Forces do to keep humanity in the corral. Without clearly understanding what has transpired in our history and how they get away with what they get away with, they will continue to distort your reality, making you think you're getting somewhere – when all along you're still "on the ranch."

CHAPTER 8

DECEPTION AND ENSLAVEMENT

"Engage people with what they expect; it is what they are able to discern and confirms their projections. It settles them into predictable patterns of response, occupying their minds while you wait for the extraordinary moment — that which they cannot anticipate."

—Sun Tzu, "The Art of War"

One of the ways that the Opponent is very effective in keeping the energy of this planet at its lowest is through deception. Deception comes in many different forms and is delivered in different packaging. According to Merriam-Webster Dictionary, deception is: "the act of making someone believe something that is not true: the act of deceiving someone." Synonyms for deception are trick, stratagem, ruse, wile, hoax, imposture.

The purpose of the deception used by those that serve Dark Forces is to provide you with an illusion of your life and the circumstances on the planet. Remember the movie, *The Truman Show*? Jim Carrey plays a man who finds out the world he is living in is just a staging of events and circumstances, dressed up as truth. Well, that is how the Dark Forces use deception on this plane: they fabricate situations, conditions and settings and make them appear real, when they are only illusions and lies. What you are experiencing is make-believe. For example, if you're engaged in watching a movie, and the scene you're observing is joyous, you may not realize that, in reality, the actors playing these joyous characters are quite hostile towards one another behind the scenes. The scene in the movie is make-believe and so is the demeanor of the characters.

On the set, the joy portrayed by those characters is an elicited emotion, created at will. It is, in actuality, a complete fabrication. An actor can pull from his memory bank and recreate the mechanics of what joy feels like and looks like: agitated speech, louder-than-usual volume, big gestures, facial expressions that demonstrate happiness, etc. Consequently, you will feel good, happy and joyful by watching others act this way. So although the joy in the scene is not real, the joy it elicits in you is real.

In the greater "set" known as this world, many things are presented to you, sold to you, which make you feel good and safe; however, in reality, they are often detrimental to you on all levels. These things may be products, services, concepts and spiritual beliefs. Those that sell you these things will tap into your feel-good centers and positive emotions, like joy, and get you to put aside any rational thoughts or objectivity that will allow you to question what is being presented. Eliciting a fraudulent "feel-good" state so you can "buy into" whatever is being sold to you is the deception.

You are living in a Matrix, a software program, hologram or astral virus put in by highly intelligent and malevolent Forces, that creates a distortion or aberration of the *Original Blueprint* of Prime Creator for all life on this planet. So many of us who serve God/The Light of Prime Creator have come into embodiment thinking that we can just hold the Light, be good, pray, be positive, meditate, have unity consciousness. In reality, though, much more is needed in order to alleviate global pain and suffering, helping shift the consciousness on the planet and helping elevate the vibration of humanity. Tackling this is a lot of work. Most of us can't even fathom the gigantic task that this involves because we've been busy trying to handle our life situations and spiritual growth. And despite all the spiritual work we've done, many of us are not where we should be in our lives. We need a lot of help ourselves.

The goal of the Dark Forces is to prevent humanity, and especially those that serve the Light of God, from reaching our maximum spiritual potential. They deceive in order to keep you in a state of perpetual confusion and stupor about the true conditions of the world you live in. They use sophisticated brainwashing techniques, delivered mostly by the media. This media provides intricate morsels of deception that elicit specific reactions or behaviors from the population.

Deception by the Media

There are many ways in which the media brainwashes us and uses deception to influence us. The media, for example, will elicit support for committing atrocities on a so-called enemy – an enemy that is conveniently created by the Opponent to justify a war. This war serves to create the illusion that there is a good side and a bad side – when it's all the same side. But the real deceit is the need to go to war, the need to intervene in other countries or police other countries. The deceit continues when we are told that there is a need to have "Big Brother-type" of surveillance systems and the need to increase the spying-power of the Government on its citizens.

The media, which is controlled by those that serve the Dark Forces, is the voice of these Forces that are currently on the planet to control the populations. The media sells you on the positive aspect of control. They tell you that the intrusion of your privacy, the extra intrusive security and the wars will keep you safe from terrorists and invasion from an enemy – the contrived and manufactured enemy. Again, this is similar to cattle getting a sense that they're safe and protected by the fences, as they graze mindlessly and roam the green pastures. All along, the fences are not there to keep danger out; they're there to keep the cattle in while they're being fattened in preparation for slaughter.

The Dark Forces create the illusion that there is a danger, and then they come up with the solution to this danger. The solution is sold to us as being in our best interest and for our protection, and/or the protection of our country. It is sold to us in a way that we believe that those putting this in place know what they're doing and have our best interest in mind. This in turn serves to dissipate any sense of fear, doubt, apprehension, stress and concerns we may have had, as we now transfer this responsibility to those who can do a better job of keeping us safe – so we think.

The solution, these reinforced fences, so to speak, elicits from us a sense of trust and safety, and also brings the feeling of relief. You're relieved because you no longer have to worry about it. You are safe from harm. Your government has your back and now you can go to work and concentrate on earning your paycheck so that you can buy the things you need, and that will make you and your family happy and comfortable. We're all doing this without realizing that we're actually in a virtual farm – just like the cows. We're not grazing; we go to work and get on the proverbial hamster wheel, too busy to notice what's really going on "behind the scenes" and too tired to care or do anything about it. And by not noticing, caring or doing anything about it, we maintain the mechanism that keeps the Matrix intact – the invisible fence that keeps us all enslaved.

ENSLAVEMENT

What does enslavement of humanity mean, exactly – after all, we're not in physical chains or behind bars or being whipped by a slave master? Enslavement is a dependence on a system or government for your wellbeing, for your existence while on this planet. It is also control – control of how you think, what you think, how you express, how you perceive, what you believe, what you feel and how you behave. You think you have control, but you don't. There are things that are not readily perceived by everyday folks because they are too busy trying to do what it takes to survive. They don't pay attention to the fine details. But if you start paying attention, you'll soon realize that we're all owned.

We have all given our power away in more ways than one, without even knowing we were doing so. Back in the day, we didn't want to do the hard labor of tilling and sowing and harvesting anymore, so we got seduced by the easier life in the big cities. We moved away from our farms, from our self-reliance and began to work in the new industries that were sprouting up like the crops we used to tend to. We exchanged our sweat for a paper that represented value – a value that fluctuated according to fictitious market conditions that no one understood and still don't understand to this day. Our bread, which we used to make from the wheat we grew, we now bought from the local store. The store depended on a truck that would bring the bread, and gas was necessary to make the truck run. When the price of gas goes up, our goods go up, and the value of the paper stays the same or diminishes.

We're on the hamster wheel of life on this planet. We lost our self-reliance because all of us wanted comfort, and some of us wanted luxury. The powers that control this world raise prices based on trade and market conditions, conditions set by the Forces that are currently in control of the planet. Those who achieve this hefty lifestyle need more money to maintain it, and to do that they often stick it to anyone who becomes a threat to their interests. The worst aspects of humanity are brought out and used for gain and power. If they own businesses that create consumer goods, they take short-cuts in quality or cut back on the quantity. They'll replace healthy ingredients with cheaper, unhealthier ones. And the consumer is unaware because they're kept busy dealing with their problems or inconsequential things – or they just don't care to know.

Unfortunately, most of humanity traded the natural life for the synthetic. Because of the nature of industry and commerce that has been established, and the "buy-in" of most citizens on the planet, we are now dependent on goods that are slowly but surely killing us with long-term illnesses. Many of us consume ingredients that are affecting our health in detrimental ways. We begin to experience symptoms whose underlying cause can't be detected by a physician's diagnosis, because they are too generic, and the culprit is a mystery. So we keep consuming that which is the cause of our demise. Products like Aspartame, MSG, Genetically Modified Foods, Refined Sugars, Fluoride, and Chlorine are amongst the detrimental products that most of us ingest and are an end-result of corporate greed.

Because these products compromise our health, and because we're under the stress of having to trade our labor in order to buy these goods, we are not being attentive to how we are being kept within a "hamster wheel". Our health is not at optimal levels, and when this happens, we lose our faith in the Unseen, in the Divine, and in those who represent the Realms of Light. We can't connect because our energy is diminished, and our vibration is lowered. We are no longer sharp with our discernment and can't tell the truth from a lie, and we can't pick up on the subtleties of deception.

And so when we're on the "spiritual path", seeking answers to our life's dilemma, and we find the teachers and spiritual leaders that melt us with their beautiful words that give us hope for a better experience here, we embrace *all of it*, without questioning, without internally searching whether what is shared is accurate. We can't connect to the Divine on our own because we're *compromised*. So we go externally to seek help. Consequently, we run into others that have been placed in leadership positions, providing us with infiltrated information that will feed us what we need to hear – the Truisms mixed with untruths.

The untruths have a very specific purpose – and that is to keep you under the illusion that you're sovereign and do as you please. The idea that you're free is a deception. As long as you think this way, you are oblivious to how you are being manipulated by these external Forces that are using you as a commodity. The Opponent and those that serve it follow certain deranged protocols that could eradicate the life forms on this planet. Some of these protocols are: 1) obtaining power by invasion of other countries and taking over natural resources, 2) control of populations by creating fear of terrorism and war, creating the need for protection, and 3) contaminating the environment and introducing new vaccines and medications, that many times create other health issues, as a response to viruses and illnesses that are by-products of greed.

What we're witnessing is a grave situation. Instead of wanting to understand what we're facing as a species, many of us – especially those who claim to serve the Light – are making the choice to not want to know. We justify why these Forces are not real. We further claim that they have been taken from this planet by the Forces of Light – information provided by the Dark Forces themselves; and yet, the evidence to the contrary is overwhelming. So we gladly embrace it as truth because we're not discerning, and it's not convenient to be aware of this and be responsible for doing something about it.

Most of the masses don't know what has transpired to cause their enslavement. Worst still, they don't even know they *are* slaves. They're oblivious of the Dark Forces that are rampant and running the planet, animating human beings in government, religion, corporations and the entertainment industry, to name a few sectors in society. Most people don't care, because they're overdosing in sugar and MSG, alcohol and drugs, and hypnotized via television, Hollywood, and the music industry. They pay for items that they can't afford and are stuck in stressful jobs just so that they can make the payments on their credit cards. If people don't realize that they're not supposed to be living a life of stress, disgust, disappointment, frustration, pain, and lament and that these conditions are imposed on them due to external, foreign and malevolent Forces, they will continue to be used as livestock so that their existence is destined to be in that hamster wheel – perpetually so.

These imposed predicaments, plus the element of competition, jealousy, gossip, rumors, greed and disdain that people display in their lives, further serves to keep the vibration at low levels. The acting out of negative emotion prevents any possibility that they'll be inclined to receive the Higher Knowledge from a book or from someone trying to elevate their awareness. It keeps them locked into the "Matrix" prison via an invisible, energetic fence that gives the impression that they are free to roam wherever they want – again, the deception.

How is the deception put into play? How is it spread? How is it maintained for so long throughout the history of mankind? Why hasn't humanity turned the tables around or wanted to? One of the reasons is the creation of religion and other belief systems that keep us in check by using fear and worship as a control mechanism.

A NEW TREND FOR HUMANITY

Maybe you give credence to the Bible and maybe you don't. Regardless of how you feel about its content and its authors, it provides an account of some of the history of humanity. We can cross-reference many of the stories in it with other sacred texts from other cultures. One of the passages that I find very interesting is Genesis 1:27 which states:

"So God created mankind in his own image, in the image of God he created them; male and female he created them."

If I am interpreting this as being literal, I can deduce that we carry God's genetics or DNA within us. Some of us can argue that the God referred to in this "creation" of humankind is no more than a demiurge or a lesser god – one that could be another race, and of extraterrestrial origin. This theory could very well be correct, but, either way, the alien race or lesser gods still harbor the Essence of Prime Creator. These also have the Original DNA and the Spark of Supreme Creator in them. So, in reality, we all have the Essence of Prime Creator, regardless how many steps and gene splicings were undertaken to derive at us.

Gematria, according to the Oxford English Dictionary is "a Kabbalistic method of interpreting the Hebrew Scriptures by computing the numerical value of words, based on the values of their constituent letters." According to Gematria, if you were to look at the original Hebrew letters, each one has a numerical value. Gregg Braden in his book *The God Code* explains that when you look at human DNA, each of the elements contained in our DNA is associated with a numerical value as well. The three main elements of

DNA are hydrogen, nitrogen, and oxygen. Using gematria, which allows us to reduce the numerical value of something to just one digit, *Hydrogen* has a number value of 1. *Nitrogen* has a number value of 5. *Oxygen* has a number value of 6. So how is God or Prime Creator encoded in our DNA? How do we know we were made in the image of Prime Creator or contain the same essence and codes? The Name of God is proof.

According to Braden, the unspoken Name, which uses only letters to represent it, is how we know. The Hebrew representation of the name of God is YHVH. The value of the Hebrew letter **Y** is 1. The value of the Hebrew letter **H** is 5. The value of the Hebrew letter **V** is 6. These three letters in Hebrew have the same numeric value as the substances that compose our DNA. Even the Arabic letters of God's name come up with the same value. This information is also found in the *Torah* and the *Sepher Yetzirah*, known as the Book of Creation, to name just two important texts.

There is a reason that the value of the elements found in our DNA and the Hebrew letters representing the name of God are the same and is not a coincidence. It is a glimpse of deliberate, intelligent Creation! Using the study of Kabbalah, along with understanding the values of the basic elements of Creation, and incorporating gematria (where the letters of major alphabets, including Greek, Coptic, Hebrew, Sanskrit, Arabic, Chinese, English, and others are given number values), we can see how Prime Creator's signature, if you will, is inscribed in our DNA.

When we set out to do this type of investigation on our own, our eyes will begin to open wide. We will be able to understand that there is a positive correlation between the values of the Hebrew letters spelling out the name of Prime Creator and that of the elements that form our DNA.

It isn't difficult to conclude that our bodies are the vehicle or the housing for our souls – it is our temple. Our bodies harbor the Divine Spark of Prime Creator and our ability to communicate directly to Source. It is to be cherished and protected, as it is used by the Creator to experience *Its* Creation through us.

There are those, though, that are currently desecrating their body-temple. There are many people who are changing their physical form via strange surgical procedures that insert horns on their heads or split their tongues in half, giving them a snake-like tongue. Some insert lenses in their eyes, making their pupils look like reptilian slits, or they'll make their eyes appear all black, with no white showing. In short, they are changing their image of being a human being to something more grotesque. The justification for this is that it's a way to express one's uniqueness. The idea that self-mutilations and permanently changing the body is a way to be unique or artistic is one of the many deceptions presented by the Opponent. You see, they want to be like Prime Creator, in that they have us look like the image of their creations – grotesqueries and aberrations of the Original and Divine Blueprint.

The body is the temple of our souls or the vessel. It was created in the Mind and Heart of Prime Creator. The body in its natural state and pristine state is designed to emulate those Beings of Light who are in direct service to Prime Creator – those who dwell closest to Zero Point. Thus, the body-temple in its pristine form is part of the Original Blueprint and Design. It has all the necessary components to harbor the Spirit of Supreme Creator. When not compromised by Negative Energies, it is radiant, vibrant, beautiful, youthful, healthy, and immortal. It is used to express the Divine Spark in the current experience and to manifest The Will of Prime Creator and All Its Glory on Earth, as well as other worlds. To mutilate it, abuse it, infect it, desecrate it, or to do the same to the bodies of others, especially children, is an abomination. It creates a seal, marking that individual as being in resonance with the Lower-Vibratory Realms.

So, one can conclude that the act of desecrating the body lowers the consciousness and the vibration. Many will fight this information, making justifications for their "choices" and stating that they own their bodies. But – I repeat – the body is sacred, it is our temple. It's the vessel that houses our soul in order to manifest the Will of Creator via our current embodiment-experience on the planet. Keeping it healthy, pristine, and free from low-vibratory thoughts, emotions, acts, and conditions – like drugs, pollutants, and toxins – is our responsibility. Ultimately, we are custodians of these bodies that harbor our eternal souls.

TRANSHUMANISM

Another aberration of humanity, created in the diabolical mind of these nefarious Forces is Transhumanism. Transhumanism is the blending of a human being's emotions, the memory and the biology with technology or machinery. Is this part of the Original and Divine Blueprint? No. It is the desecration and hijacking of the Original Design. Here are some examples of what Transhumanism aims to accomplish, according to the World Transhumanist Association: uploading of our consciousness into a virtual reality; personality pills; lifelong emotional well-being through recalibration of the pleasure centers; artificial intelligence and vastly extended lifespans; and enhanced health via manipulation at the cellular level through nanotechnology. These are just a few examples of what Transhumanism is trying to accomplish.

Some of this sounds incredibly promising. It is challenging to find fault with a technology that gives us hope; improved health; expanded lifespan, and the ability to preserve our memories, boost our intelligence and more. The Dark Forces that are inspiring this Transhumanism agenda are attempting to create their version of humanity. They are also degrading the Original, Master Blueprint for mankind created by Prime Creator; because, in this *Original Blueprint*, humanity is Superior to anything created thus far. This technology aims at taking away the ability for Self-Mastery since this robotic-integration does it for you – up to a point. So, you're not mastering "Self" because real Mastery is acquired through choices, using free will.

The merging with technology to correct things that we can correct on our own through conscious effort and Self-Mastery makes the individual more focused on physicality in this third-dimensional reality, instead of spirituality. Therefore, achieving Self/Spiritual Mastery would intrinsically provide freedom from all human limitations in this realm.

Another drawback with merging with machines is that it would inhibit our desire for direct connection to God/Source for our transformation into the Perfect Beings we were designed to be. Instead, this new science and those behind it are enticing us with integrated technology that will give us the cure to our ailments and eradicate the limitations that have been created and imposed by these Dark Forces. So, again, they create the problem and then provide the solution, this time via technology – that becomes the answer to our current experience of limitation and suffering.

And what is the "grand plan" of these master-minds of deception and darkness? They want to create their version of humanity: the New Adam, the New Eve. They are crowning themselves as another "Prime Creator" in their own hell world and want to take this new creation and the new technological advancements that go with it, into the Cosmos to defile other intelligent life-forms. Again, it's the bad science experiment, the pathological virus crawling out of the petri dish and infecting everything in the lab.

You may have already awoken to the fact that religion is not what it claims itself to be. Religion cannot be equated with spirituality. The former is dogmatic, run by mortals who claim to have the inspiration of the God that "wrote" the texts dictating how we must behave in order to enter the Kingdom of Heaven. The latter should connect you directly to The Supreme Creator – The All That Is – and bypasses all intermediaries and all interpretation, disinformation, lies, and manipulation of Illumined Truth. The former makes you dependent, separating you from direct communion with your True Creator. The latter unifies all of us and embraces the fact that we are all Sparks of Divine, Source-Creator. The former separates, labels, condemns and creates atrocities in the name of "God" in order to advance its agenda. The latter embraces our diversity, loves, forgives, uplifts and respects all life. The problem is, as you might expect at this low-vibratory level, that spirituality too has been infiltrated and hijacked, creating dangerous traps for the non-discerning!

CHAPTER 9

THE NEW AGE MOVEMENT

"If you know the enemy and know yourself, you need not fear the result of a hundred battles. If you know yourself but not the enemy, for every victory gained you will also suffer a defeat. If you know neither the enemy nor yourself, you will succumb in every battle."

—Sun Tzu, "The Art of War"

I f you've done research on spiritual topics, you probably know by now that the self-imposed "rulers" of this world – all archontic influence, entities, djinn, demons, negative ETs (collectively, Dark Forces) – have their hands in every "movement" on this planet. But what you may not know is that it's much more sinister than that. They actually *create* these movements using human beings who have already been compromised by them, who are already in allegiance with them.

Who are these people? Most of the "candidates" are actors and musicians, government and corporate officials, and religious and spiritual leaders. Charming, persuasive, "respectable", admired, and famous, these folks have made themselves accessible to the Darker

Energies by choosing to engage in behaviors, thoughts and/or emotions that are conducive to lower vibration. So, whatever "inspiration" or directive these people are getting, they're not receiving it from The Divine or Highest Source, but from representatives of realms that are heinous and execrable. These dark and nefarious representatives are "soul-whisperers", providing information in such a way that seems to be coming from benign sources or Representatives of the Higher Realms. The messages are "gift-wrapped" with beautiful choices of words and phraseology and, of course... the Truisms. Those that are recruited – unbeknownst to them – can't discern what is going on. Their "B.S." detector isn't functioning... or they've turned it off. They are simply physical shells, bodies that have become animated by the whim of Dark Forces.

Introducing the Deceit

For those not familiar with The New Age Movement, it is a spiritual mishmash of different religions, philosophies and pearls of wisdom. The movement draws material from various sources, including but not limited to: Theosophy; the Ancient Mystery Schools; Rosicrucian; Metaphysics; Kabbalistic Mysticism; Christianity; the Law of Attraction; Gnosticism; Neopaganism; Toltec Wisdom; Buddhism; Hinduism and Yoga, to name just a few. Intrinsically, this information allows us to recognize our connection with God and each other. It enables us to feel interconnected with all living things. It facilitates a deep relationship with Earth, making her the focal point of our spiritual connection since she is the life-giver and source of our existence. New Age "spirituality" is a potpourri of ideologies and beliefs where the underlying message is that we're God. The assortment of philosophies and ideas provide us with the desire to unite with one another; that is, when we're not arguing in defense of our beliefs and points of view.

In reality, the New Age Movement is like a net. It catches all the defectors from formalized religion and provides a feel-good platform for those seeking out Truth. The new spiritual philosophies resonate in your heart, and they allow you to experience a feeling of ease and peace because your soul recognizes truth behind the concepts. And there lies the danger.

The thing is that this Movement, along with formalized religion, was conceived and implemented by the Dark Forces. They know most of us are already jaded and fed up with the traditional religious beliefs, so they offer us an alternative, keeping us placated. In reality, however, this is just another way for them to reel us in further. That, unfortunately, is the crux of the New Age Movement-Campaign with its glorious concepts and lavish Truisms. The Negative Forces skillfully disguise a lie in the same message as the Truism – like someone might disguise a bitter medicine within a candy or marshmallow.

If you've ever had a dog, you'll understand the following analogy. I am the proud owner of a Golden Retriever. She's highly allergic and often gets infections from scratching. The medicine I have to give her is bitter. She totally hates it. She also loves marshmallows, though, so I hide the pill inside a marshmallow. First, I give her a plain marshmallow, which immediately gets her tail wagging in excitement. She wolfs it down, then sits and looks from me to the marshmallow bag, eagerly waiting for more. Now I place the bitter pill inside a marshmallow and give it to her. She savors the marshmallow and in her excitement swallows the pill as well. She may taste the pill, but because the marshmallow cuts the bitterness, she decides to ignore it and just enjoy the sweet treat. She happily swallows the marshmallow and the bitter pill – two separate components that were forced together to form one treat. Had the bitter pill been given separately, my dog would not have taken it at all.

In the case of the New Age Movement, the Truism is the "spiritual marshmallow" hiding the bitter lie or the deception. It is the packaging, the showcasing, and the marketing that makes the concepts alluring. It's like the clever commercial conceived by Madison Avenue advertising geniuses – designed to appeal to your emotions, your senses, your dreams, your "hot buttons".

Let's say, for example, that you suffer from insomnia, and it's making you miserable. One day you just happen to see a television commercial for a certain medication that can help alleviate this. It shows a sleeping woman who is finally getting much-needed rest. She wakes up refreshed and ready to tackle the world. The pictures that are used to convey this message are beautiful, the music is exquisite and the actress portrays a person who is rested, has vitality, is in joy and is attractive and healthy. She has all of this because she can finally sleep due to this amazing medication – and this sounds like the answer to your prayers.

You now begin to pay close attention to the commercial. You too want to be able to sleep. You have a need to feel good, and a desire to be attractive, joyful and healthy. Because this message addresses your needs and resonates with you, your guard goes down. It's almost as if the commercial was written specifically for you – it addresses your situation perfectly. You get caught up in the emotion of hope, and your objectivity goes out the window.

Then, in the background you hear a low, rapid voice listing all the things the medicine could cause: severe abdominal cramps, vision impairment, dizziness, bleeding of the gums, severe migraines, blood clots, lowered blood pressure, and heart failure. You may not even pay attention to the disclaimer, because you're so mesmerized by the overall positive, feel-good message that you desperately want to hear – and so desperately want to believe.

Maybe you do hear the disclaimer and don't care about the consequences because the benefits outweigh any and all repercussions. You are making a choice to either not use your discernment or to not pay attention to it. This discernment comes in the form of a feeling or nudging in your gut – one that is trying to warn you to pay attention, yet you discard.

The Dark Forces are also engaged in marketing campaigns, and their goal is to dupe humanity. Like the television commercial, they are very cleverly designed and executed, so that most of us, especially those that serve the Light, are not aware of how we're being played and used. The Dark Forces know which words, pictures, ideas, and concepts will spike your interest, keep your attention, lower your guard, illicit certain behaviors, stroke your ego, and reconstruct your belief-system. They are also adept at keeping you from getting direct information from Source by making you feel "less than" or spiritually unworthy or – even worse – spiritually needy. This way, you have to continue getting your "truths" from the unscrupulous disinformation brokers, such as compromised spiritual leaders, teachers, gurus, and channelers. The more you go externally for spiritual information, the less empowered you feel, which makes you seek even more external spiritual information – thus perpetuating the vicious cycle of the disinformation campaign.

If you are not anchored in your heart, connecting with your Divine *"Knowing"* and functioning with full discernment, you get suckered into the propaganda presented by these vile Forces. And before you know it, you begin to regurgitate – verbatim – the lie. This type of brainwashing is a tactic used by Communist factions to take over countries. It's a way to get the people to buy into the revolutionary rhetoric. As in the case of the television commercial, you are so enthralled by the beautiful pictures that you throw common sense out the window. You would probably even recommend the medicine to friends and family, ignoring or downplaying the negative side effects because of its alleged health benefits. In this case, you'd be using what's called selective discernment. It means that you decide to ignore inconsistencies in a message because you feel that the overall message is sound, and your need for the outcome is greater than the need to avert any possible harm.

LOWERING YOUR GUARD

As mentioned previously, the New Age Movement wraps the disinformation in seemingly benign Truisms, which makes it more palatable to you. You let your guard down. You stop being vigilant. You rationalize that this movement is about Truth, Love, Peace, Harmony, and Unity Consciousness – it's about our Ascension. You come in completely open and receptive, like an empty vessel waiting to be filled. But filled with what? When the information comes in, you take it *all* in – truth mixed with untruths. You devour it all, like the pill in the marshmallow. You don't detect the lies and/or you make a conscious decision that the lies, like the bitter medicine, are tolerable and are a means to an end – getting the missing tidbits of information you need for spiritual wellness.

On the other hand, even if you do catch the lie, you might infer that the lie must be Truth. You doubt your discernment because you have become needy; you believe you're not spiritually worthy. This skewed perception of yourself – placed there by the clever and disparaging Dark Forces – is further strengthened by the stock you place on the source disseminating the information. Is the source of this information a well-known individual, a reputable teacher, a respected spiritual leader, a channeler whose information is posted on every website and forwarded via email? Who is the messenger or spiritual-celebrity that is being used to deliver the "disinformation brew"? The importance placed on this messenger plays a huge factor in how you perceive the message and how it gets you to lower your guard and put your discernment aside. The result is that your mind is infiltrated with a new set of beliefs that will steer you – and others – down a wrong, long and bumpy path towards disempowerment.

As a consequence, you start embracing concepts and behaviors that make you think you're in service to others when in reality you're in service to self or worse, the Dark Forces. You begin to emulate the speech and the behavior patterns of those who share this lovely new path. You become so consumed by "self" and your personal well-being – which includes but is not limited to your meditations and chants, workshops and sweat lodges, incense-burning and all the tchotchkes that are involved in your rituals and ceremony – that you begin to ignore the world around you. And while you're busy looking at the beautiful carrot – namely, the promise of an Ascension – that has been placed in front of you, the Opponent is advancing in a very organized, stealthy and focused manner.

IT SOUNDS RIGHT

Part of the tactics of the Dark Forces is to have spiritual leaders, authors, teachers and channelers in the New Age community disseminate beautifully packaged disinformation. They also distort a Truism so that it is used indiscriminately and blindly. Some of these include, "I create my reality"; "that which we put our attention to we manifest"; "we are getting help from Angelic Beings"; "we will be rescued by ETs"; "the bank gangsters (or banksters) are being arrested"; "the evil-doers are losing ground"; "all the Dark Forces and entities, including all negative ETs, have been taken from the planet".

These ideas and statements make sense to you, and after hearing them often enough, you start using them to explain away everything in your physical reality – without discernment or truly understanding the concept. You then share this watered down version with others, spreading it like a disease and further eroding everyone's ability to discern. And because you trust the source, you figure you don't need to use your discernment anyway.

Disinformation includes the made up "rescue missions" and interventions that make you believe that everything will be taken care of by external sources. These types of lies ultimately inhibit you from stepping into your Power. And because having someone else take care of your dirty work is the "path of least resistance" (and releases you from any responsibility), you gladly embrace the lie. This further weakens your perception and discernment skills, and before long, the lie becomes your new truth. Although the outer world doesn't reflect what the New Age propaganda claims, you cannot see it through your new perception filters!

Why is this important to understand? Why are the Dark Forces creating this deception? They want to get you comfortable. They want you to have a false sense of security and a feeling that everything is fine. They want you to think everything is being taken care of by ETs, Archangels, Ascended Masters, Elohim, etc., so there is nothing you need to do or worry about. You now go about with your business, and before you know it you have become complacent, apathetic, disengaged, disconnected and indifferent. In the meantime, the things in the world that you came to help change are becoming worse – because no one is minding the store. Aren't the Dark Forces clever? On the other hand, the Light Forces have not been very good at Spiritual Warfare in this realm. We're easily fooled.

Positive ETs, real Archangels, real Ascended Masters, the true Elohim and other High-Vibratory Beings of Light in service to Prime Creator are vigilant and cognizant of what is transpiring at this low-vibratory plane of existence. Every so often they will intervene when necessary, especially for one of their Emissaries or Ambassadors. But it is our responsibility, as custodians of this planet, to clean up the mess. We need to be the Masters that we are and take charge of the situation that has gone out of control on this planet. It has escalated on our watch. I've often wondered why this is. Maybe we think we're doing a magnificent job, and the Dark Forces are standing down. The funny thing is that the Dark Forces are counting on this very form of delusion and arrogance, because this is what is keeping us in submission.

PHYSICALITY

We're in a bodysuit at this moment to do a job. It is no different than those folks who work in a biological lab and suit up to protect themselves against dangerous pathogens. When the task is done, they unsuit and go home. In this embodiment, you are wearing a suit comprised of skin, bones, muscles, veins and arteries, etc., which also carries a genetic lineage from your ancestors that makes you look, think, express and feel the way you do. You use this bodysuit to experience your world and to allow you to blend with the others – who also wear similar suits – so that you can get the job done in this bigger "lab" called Earth.

It may be hard to believe, but you came into physicality to do much more than just seek your spiritual graduation in the form of the Rapture or Ascension. Your graduation is a natural process once you've been fully immersed in physicality – with all its challenges – and have made the right choices, been in service-to-others, and can Master all your emotions, thoughts, physical limitations and spiritual derailments. Eventually, and as a consequence, your consciousness will shift, expand and infuse itself with God-Consciousness, allowing you to experience as God experiences. That level of consciousness is attained through Self-Mastery.

Your incarnation in this world is therefore also used to uplift others, encourage them and help raise awareness. It is by being in physicality, immersing yourself completely in this expression, that you have the capabilities of transforming conditions and experiences on this planet that are not in alignment with the Higher-Vibratory Frequencies of the Kingdom of God, also known as the Illumined Realms of Prime Creator.

Also, in order to achieve your graduation from a third-dimensional density, you need to be fully engaged in service-to-others. You can't be in service-to-others if you're not *fully* aware of what is going on around the planet or *wholly* engaged in seeking ways to correct what is not in alignment with the Original Blueprint of Prime Creator. You should begin by shaking off the dust from your garment of Light, which serves as evidence of your Mastery, and then stepping into your Divine Power and Authority. It is the time to realize who you are, in truth, and reclaim your spiritual inheritance. It is time to put down the "spiritual entertainment" and distractions found on websites, in chat rooms and at gatherings and get serious about what you're here to accomplish. It is time to make your voice heard, and your presence known. It is time to get to work and start making a difference on all levels that pertain to this world. You cannot just be a bystander and backseat driver anymore, allowing things to get worse and allowing the Dark Forces to have full reign.

Wishing things will get better or using visualization techniques alone won't work – it takes physicality to put it into action! Looking away is not an option, especially for those who have come in as Light Emissaries and Masters from The Illumined Realms with a commitment to being fully present and in full participation. These people carry a heavier responsibility and burden, and when they are apathetic, indifferent or disengaged it carries universal repercussions. This type of disengagement and non-participation is precisely what the Dark Forces have instilled in most of us via the new, false spiritual practices.

Instead of continuing to engage in these self-indulgent practices, we need to behave in effective, spiritually responsible and mature ways. We need to understand that an embodiment means just that – to in-body. Why bother to be in a body if we don't need it to do our work? Indeed, why bother to embody into this dense world at all if it isn't to help uplift it – and to allow us to choose correctly, based on the challenges we face? Again, we take form in order to help bring about the changes that need to occur in a world – changes that cannot be accomplished unless the Higher-Vibratory Realms have physical representatives to carry out The Plan. At this stage of the game, that Plan is for the Light Emissaries to be catalysts for change so that Higher Consciousness can be seeded, and so the vibration of humanity can be escalated. A virus has infected this realm, and we are the antidote. It takes all of us to be aware of this and use our physical bodies to anchor The Plan of Creator.

Remember, we are the custodians of this world, and, as such we need to stop focusing so much on ourselves and start figuring out how we can fix this mess. The desire, passion, and drive to make this happen will generate a momentum of positive, creative energy that in and of itself will help propel change. It will also increase our vibratory rate since we'll be involved with selfless acts of kindness and compassion toward all Life on the planet. The raising of our consciousness and vibratory rate will help in our Ascension from this lower-density, propelling us to those higher octaves or planes of existence that we remember and desire to reach again. In other words, our graduation or shift of consciousness happens automatically when we are not thinking of ourselves, but of others; when the ultimate goal is not what we're aspiring for ourselves, but what we aspire for others. Then we would have the greatest of rewards – to see another achieve their personal spiritual transformation and liberation from this Matrix.

BEING ON THE SAME PAGE

If we don't all share the same vision of a better world and have the same goal of helping others earn their freedom from this Matrix, we won't be effective! This truth reminds me of a quote from Mark 3:25 – *"And if a house be divided against itself, that house cannot stand"*. We are that house that is divided against itself. As mentioned previously, humanity, especially those who serve The Light, are easily manipulated, and our energies quickly dispersed. We have more opinions among us than we know what to do with; we're also on information overload, which tends to pull us in many directions. We, as a spiritual collective, share a common goal – that elusive and nebulous Ascension. Other than that, we're all dancing to our own tune.

We cannot personally progress when we're in ego, misperceiving, misinterpreting, getting wounded emotionally, thinking we're victims, and blaming others. We cannot attain Christ/God-Consciousness when we're hating individuals or groups of people and instigating others to do the same. We cannot transform ourselves or the world when we're having to defend our beliefs and when we're having to cling to truths and philosophies that either hold us back or cannot be supported, especially considering the overwhelming evidence to the contrary. How do we expand our consciousness if we display spiritual arrogance and irresponsibility? We need to realize that there are many of us, millions of us, claiming to serve The Light and Prime Creator and just about as many philosophies about how to get back "Home".

We need to look closer at what's causing this lack of unity. There are a couple of observations that we can make: 1) there are multiple realities (this is actually correct to a point and could explain why there are so many opinions and philosophies); 2) we have all been fed information that strikes our personal fancy, keeping us sated and happy and within the confines of our comfort zone, as we view our circumstances and the world through these philosophical lenses; 3) we hold onto our point of view regardless of what evidence there is against it; 4) we're being manipulated by external Dark Forces that feed us erroneous information that resonates with our personal truth.

The Opponent is aware of your beliefs regarding Ascension. It also knows what your idea of a Fifth-Dimensional Earth looks like, what humanity will be like, and what the Kingdom of Heaven feels like. These Forces fabricate that place and replay it on the movie screen of your mind. They even put mental "road signs" for you, with messages like: "It's only five more years away"; "you have to keep up the fifteen-hour meditations"; "keep attending those workshops"; " you need the latest channeled message"; and so on. These help maintain you on the path to your goal. They are designed to set your eyes on the "prize" – arriving at your version of utopia.

What if everyone has an exclusive commercial of utopia playing in their head, and the roadmap to get there is provided by your local, "archontic" travel agency? Your destination is so real and palpable that there is no way anyone else's version or roadmap is correct. You feel you are privileged to receive confidential information on how to get to this exclusive paradise. And this is a delusion that keeps you thinking you're correct, and others are wrong.

BOASTING AND MASTERY

Why would you need to prove to anyone who has a slightly different perspective or insight into spirituality that your point of view is better or that your spiritual path is the best one, or that you are a Master, or that you're on the verge of Ascension? In reality, a real Master doesn't divulge he is a Master. He doesn't boast. He just is.

Being a Master is not a badge that is worn, especially externally. It is a level of attainment, and that accomplishment is carried internally. An individual that has attained this spiritual level will exert Mastery over himself, which includes his behavior, his thoughts, his lower emotions, and his choices. A Master doesn't label himself or others. He is Neutral, Objective and in a perpetual state of Equanimity. A real Master is Meek and Humble, yet wields the sword of Truth and Righteousness, if need be.

Let's explore the spiritual meaning of "meek". When the word "meek" is used in the New Testament, for example, and then is translated into Greek, the word used for "meek" is *prautes* (πραΰτης). This term connotes a total lack of self-pride and lack of self-concern. It also denotes humility for one's personal predicament and puts the focus on self-less service. It signifies a gentleness in character that quenches the fire of anger in others.

Another Greek word for meek is *praus* (πραΰς), which means a mildness of disposition, gentleness of spirit, meekness or a strength of spirit, a disciplined calmness. It is a contrast to anger, arrogance and self-absorption. It defines a person who is not only exerting calmness but is demonstrating a compassionate service to others. And according to BibleHub.com, it also means showing power without undue harshness.

So if you witness bickering and animosity based on differences of opinion, especially different philosophical or spiritual points of view, and one of the parties is boasting about their attainment or Spiritual Mastery, this should sound alarms for you. Maybe you'll start asking yourself whether the behavior you're witnessing is an example of Mastery. You could also ask what's behind this type of behavior and why does it occur.

YOUR VULNERABILITY

I hope you understand by now that these Dark Forces are also masters. They are masters of deception; masters of luring; masters of creating chaos and animosity; masters in keeping your vibration low; masters of propaganda and marketing; and masters of dividing us. What is their aim, besides giving us a false sense of security? One of their many goals is to prevent us from being unified so that we're easily conquered. Their ultimate plan is an all-out takeover of humanity, and if you're not on to this, there will come a point of no return – a point when even if we are all in agreement and on the same page for once, their momentum and the damage incurred would be too difficult to overcome.

There are no External Forces coming to the rescue, as many firmly believe. You and I are those Forces; and we have been decommissioned, hypnotized and put in a stupor by the cleverness of the Opponent – who knows that we are too trustworthy and willing to go to external sources for our answers and then go to war with each other over differences of opinion. The Opponent knows us better than we know ourselves, and it is highly skilled at Spiritual Warfare. It knows the true meaning of unity. The Opponent takes full advantage of our weaknesses to further its agenda, and the Forces in its service are ready, willing and able to do whatever it takes to win this Spiritual War.

To recap, you and I are easily tricked because we seek the answers to the Truth *outside ourselves*. The sources we have used to get these Truths have been infiltrated by the Dark Forces, which provide the Truisms mixed in with the disinformation. The disinformation is embraced without question, and the lie now becomes a part of our philosophy and belief system, which makes us defend it by arguing and having discord with others. The dispute leads to separation and negative emotions, which in turn lowers our vibratory rate.

How do we reach the Higher-Vibratory Realms when our vibration is low? We can't. Thus, we remain trapped in a low-vibratory state, a lower density plane of existence – as they use our arrogance, resentment and disdain as an "energy drink". The disinformation further serves to create a state of complacency and false security. And in doing so, it thwarts our desire to engage in implementing solutions to planetary situations that impact all life. It is an intelligent, self-replicating, self-serving, diabolical plan that has replaced the Divine one – and it is happening right under our noses!

CHAPTER 10

THE TRUTH MOVEMENT

*"To capture the enemy's entire army is better than to destroy it; to
take intact a regiment, a company, or a squad is better than to
destroy them. For to win one hundred victories in one hundred
battles is not the supreme of excellence. To subdue the enemy
without fighting is the supreme excellence."*

—Sun Tzu, "The Art of War"

The Truth Movement was birthed in order to accommodate the
defectors of the New Age Movement. Why were there defectors, you ask? Many began practicing partial discernment and saw
that the conditions occurring on the planet did not jive with what
they were being fed by the New-Agers. Many of the so-called spiritual teachers were forecasting Ascension and a Fifth-Dimensional
Earth by the Winter Solstice of 2012. Some predicted mass landings of ET Spacecraft, while others talked about Angels, Benevolent
ETs and other Beings of Light coming to assist in clearing up the
mess – events that didn't occur, especially within the timeline they
predicted.

This type of hype and disinformation was circulated on most spiritual radio talk shows, YouTube channels, blogs, websites, social media, in books and spiritual workshops. When none of it happened, it caused a lot of disillusion and disappointment. Worse than that was the negative effect of the false information – it had induced the stagnation of the advancement of the Light on the planet because it caused false hope, false security, and false victory. We wasted valuable time and energy predicting, projecting, and imagining an event that would catapult us out of here. We became dependent on the latest channeled messages from various ET groups or off-world councils that were filling us in on the updates – keeping us hanging at the edge of our seat, like a good thriller. When the dates that were predicted came to pass and nothing transpired, the timeline would be moved. The explanation given was that these Beings that were channeled had moved the event or that we had made such progress that it was no longer necessary to have YXZ happen.

As a result, many of the New-Agers started getting a bad taste in their mouths and began to question. They began to notice inconsistencies. They realized they were being lied to and that this act of lying was orchestrated by none other than the Nefarious Forces, currently in control of this dimension. These New Age Movement defectors scrambled for answers and found that there were many others out there who were also bailing. This insurgency spawned The Truth Movement, whose aim was to get to the bottom of the fakery – and to expose the evildoers behind the scenes that were creating situations and scenarios that could ultimately lead to the extermination of humanity. In short, those in the Truth Movement were out to eradicate everything that was given as truth by the New Age Movement and was going to expose it as fraud.

"Truth" leaders emerged and soon became the heroes to all the former New-Agers now rushing to them for spiritual insight. Much of the information being disseminated by this new movement focused on exposing evil controllers and putting faces behind them.

These overseers, the Truthers claimed, were helping to commit evil deeds against humanity, deeds that were conceived and designed by an extraterrestrial race known as Reptilians. However, this too was overly generalized because it was putting the total blame on the wrong group.

Assuming this was true, that the Reptilians were the root of the evil and enslavement of humanity, why were more of these new leaders not asking questions like, "What controls the Reptilians?" or "Who do they serve?" There were some theories thrown around (not necessarily by the new leaders), that the Archons (or rulers, according to the Nag Hammadi Library) have dominion over the Reptilians. But my question is, who controls the Archons? Not many in the Truth Movement were asking this question or digging deeper.

So, a new craze started – a "witch hunt" – about spotting Reptilians in the media, in government, in Buckingham Palace, in Hollywood, and in the music industry – even the Vatican. YouTube was full of clips showing government officials, Hollywood stars, news anchors and British Royalty shape-shifting in front of cameras. This inquisition is still evident and on the rise. There is much evidence that creatures, which are not human and *not* in alignment with The Plan of Prime Creator, are influencing the leaders of religious institutions, the entertainment industry, large corporations, and governments. They also seem to have a thirst for human suffering and human blood. Child trafficking, pedophilia, and satanic rituals committed by many leaders of religious institutions, governments, and diverse industries are prevalent, escalating, beyond sick and disturbing. But what appoints these creatures and what animates them? By now, I think it is easy to formulate conclusions about that…

ASTRAL SPIN DOCTORS

Let's pretend I'm running for office. People don't like me much. They think that I'm shady, and I have a lot of skeletons in my closet, and they know I have had questionable business dealings with unethical corporations that are greedy and compromising human lives by cutting corners. I support them because they are high contributors to my campaign. I've been caught receiving bribes. Yep, I'm corrupt. I have just been exposed again by the media and have a good chance of losing this campaign. My main opponent is a "darling", according to the eyes of the public. He can do no wrong and is the favorite to win this race. I know he knows the same people I do and has dealt with them on a social level.

So, because I'm unscrupulous, shrewd, conniving, callous, sinister, and calculating, I come up with a master plan of deception. I will expose myself. I will confess to everything publically, revealing my corruption, all my ill-doings and others who had anything to do with it. Now that everyone knows how bad I am, I will implicate my opponent in the corruption by linking his name with my cohorts and shady business partners. I will even generate emails, doctor photos or create fake purchase orders as evidence.

People will start questioning him now. They'll ask why he's done business with these "dirty" corporations or why he's had any dealings with them and why he's covered it up. It will make him lose favor until he's no longer seen as the "political darling". He will lose votes because of the perceived shadiness and corruption. I'm betting that the negative publicity I've helped to generate will cause people to doubt his character. I'm hoping that because I came clean that they would start to trust me, but even if they don't, that's fine because they won't trust him either. That way, I can still be in the game while he's busy trying to put out the fires that are damaging his reputation. The aim is to make him lose his momentum and his advantage while I pick up some of his voters. Being skilled at the art of deception, I created the illusion that my opponent wasn't trustworthy by spinning the story that originally implicated me.

Similarly, those claiming to be the "masters" of this world – the Opponent or Dark Forces – have astutely positioned themselves to reap the benefits of their deception. They point fingers at their minions and even at themselves, as a way to get you believing you're on the "right track". Thus, these masters of Psyop were the ones that created the Truth Movement. This movement now became another platform to introduce more disempowering *disinformation*, pulling out the net yet again to haul in all those disgusted with the New Age Movement. And thus the deceit continues, by presenting the case that the New Age Movement was compromised by Reptilians, Archons, Dark Lords, Satanic Forces, Entities, Djinn, etc., and that these have infiltrated everything, and that it's all controlled by these fallen beings.

Please take notice of how clever they are, how there is always a purpose behind their efforts – since in this basket of Fallen Entities and Dark Forces they have also included Ascended Masters, Archangels, Elohim, Benevolent ETs, Angels and any Being that works directly with Prime Creator to uphold The Light and restore balance. These Dark Forces expose themselves, and their minions, by leaking information about how they're involved in humanity's demise; and at the same time they implicate their opposition – The Light Forces – as being a part of this scheme. Isn't that a kicker? You must admit that they have thought of everything… and that they're very impressive! They are so efficient that they utilize specific, influential individuals to introduce these concepts; this makes the lie more credible and allows them to spread it more quickly.

Their plan would be thwarted if so many of us weren't buying into it. It is time for us to start using our discernment and take responsibility for what is taking place in this reality. When we're in agreement with the *disinformation*, when we become complacent and do nothing, it sends out a clear message that we're giving our consent to their interference and manipulation; to the desecration of this world and our enslavement.

What is the Opponent trying to accomplish here? The purpose of this particular disinformation campaign is to discredit the True Beings of Light and to steer you away from them. It is meant to dissuade you from working with them or emulating them – especially if doing so will expand your consciousness, increase your vibration, and empower you. This campaign is skillfully designed to raise suspicion about all the Emissaries of Light that are off-planet – the True Emissaries, the True Beings of Light that serve humbly behind the scenes to help humanity. These legitimate Light Beings work diligently to bring the Will and Plan of Prime Creator to the planet, trying to restore the balance, as per the Original Blueprint.

Clearly, it's not in the best interest of these Dark Forces for us to be learning from those who have achieved true Mastery and liberation. The problem here is that you can't be truly discerning if you're trying to work with preconceived ideas given to you by the Negative Forces. If you discern in this manner, you will look at everything based on the pair of glasses they gave you – which can only capture *their* skewed reality. You need to use your higher Discernment, with a capital "D". You need to step out of the witch-hunt-drama or the "hype" of the Truth Movement. You also need to approach the information from a much higher perspective, and understand the mindset and tactics of the Opponent. So Discernment is the best tool to get to the Real Truth. But this requires razor-sharp objectivity and good judgment, one that many of us have either not yet acquired or have allowed to atrophy. It also involves one more thing – connecting directly to Source/Prime Creator to get the correct information.

FAKE ASCENDED MASTERS AND BEINGS OF LIGHT

Have the Dark Forces infiltrated the Ascended Masters, Archangels, Angels, and Benevolent ET races? Of course not! These Higher-Vibratory Beings by their very nature and Higher Consciousness cannot be compromised, especially because they are in High-Vibratory states and Mastery. They are predisposed to serve the Light and as a consequence, they possess God-Consciousness and are at the Highest Vibratory level possible for their current expression. So, those Higher-Vibratory Beings who reside in the realms closest to the Bosom of Creator cannot be lured, tempted, compromised, infiltrated, deceived or duplicated. They cannot be duplicated because of their energy signature and vibration. These are unique to each of these Beings of Light. The problem is that this frequency-identifier is only evident to those that are also of higher vibration and have had personal interaction with these Beings before. Being in high vibration is how we can perceive and recognize the refined and subtle electronic field.

Most people can't perceive this electronic field; the Dark Forces make sure of that when they keep us in low vibration. Then they create a bad copy of the Beings of Light, especially the well-known ones. They're counting on the fact that if you desire an experience with these Beings and you've never had one before, you will never know the difference between a real one and an impostor, because you have nothing to compare the experience with. And, they figure that you will be so overwhelmed with joy and awe that you will feel privileged to have this experience with those that are connected to the Higher Realms.

So just like with a Broadway show, they set out to recreate an elaborate production. The makeshift Ascended Masters and other false Beings of Light, present themselves in beautiful, youthful bodies. They wear robes made out of refined material; they are radiant, and their beautiful blue eyes emit pure love. The Dark Forces, these "playwrights" of the Matrix, fabricate what we believe to be the look, speech, behavior and demeanor of what the Spiritual Community deems to be an Ascended Master, Archangel or benign extraterrestrial. This cast of impostors presents themselves with total composure, peace, compassion, love, and assertiveness – a performance that can easily win an Academy Award.

The speech and demeanor are usually contrived, made to fit your notion of what this should be like. Unfortunately, it is all fantasy. It is a projection placed in your mind – by the Opponent – of the fabricated comportment of an Ascended Master or other Being of Light. When you encounter a fake one, it's a match with what you expected and, therefore, accept it as real. They fulfill your expectation of what these Ascended Masters look like and sound like based on stories and folklore – all written by them, of course – in anticipation for a future Psyop. So, they set up the "con job" way in advance so that you have a predisposition to accept the fakes.

If you are faced with one of these imposters, whether in person or through channeled material, you automatically assume it's an Ascended Master or a Being that represents The Light. You blindly adhere to their teachings and messages without question – you take the marshmallow. You believe that the Being standing in front of you, or giving you messages via a channeler, is who he says he is. You automatically grant him "Master" status or a status of authority. You fall for the fakery and the trickery because the Being uses terms of endearment and is good at talking "the talk". It gives you words that you are accustomed to hearing in the New Age and other Spiritual Movements that carry positive connotations.

The use of these buzz words has been identified by the Opponent as eliciting specific reactions from you. In this case it involves lowering your guard, putting aside discernment and implicitly embracing the impostors and their messages. I call this type of a buzz word "fluff". They use it to embellish their speeches and messages to make them more alluring, more impressive. You then assume they're saying something important, meaningful and life-altering – when all along they're not saying anything that you don't already know. They just say it in a pretty way. They use Truisms – again, to obscure the lies that they are making you swallow in order to disempower you.

By presenting you with this extravagant show, they convince you that they are Beings of The Light and in service to Prime Creator. These impostors will usually announce themselves as Master such-and-such, or Lord such-and-such or use the familiar name of an Archangel or Ascended Master to show legitimacy. They're great at name-dropping. They can even fabricate a name that sounds like it is befitting of a Being of Light. And, unfortunately, those of us that are hungry for this type of encounter will eat this up! You too will fall for this because you want to believe they're real. You will get bamboozled, just like you would if you were to buy a "lemon" from a slick used-car salesperson.

The impostors will stroke your ego, telling you how wonderful and loved you are, how in joy they are that you are being of service to humanity and the Light. They show gratitude that you're working diligently to help in Earth's Ascension, and they reassure you that they are here to help, and everything is under control. Then they begin to introduce the Truisms, and in your mind you're nodding yes to every word. You feel so loved, so much peace and safety. Their words ring true in your heart and resonate with you because you are familiar with this truth. It takes no time before they start dispensing the bitter pill, the disinformation – strategically positioned within the mélange of cleverly selected words that make the message palatable. Once you bring down your defenses, usually in the form of your discernment, you now become the carrier of the disinformation virus that will now be spread to others through your emails, blogs, social media, internet videos, lectures and workshops.

So are there false Ascended Masters, false Archangels, false Angels, false benevolent ETs and false Councils? Yes and No. Yes, there are impersonators or deceptive-versions or wannabes animated by the Dark Forces whose job is to deceive you. And no, because the real and true Ascended Masters and other Beings in service to The Light of Prime Creator and All Creation do not lure; do not deceive; do not need to impress; do not need to be worshipped; do not need to speak using buzz words or fluff; they do not embellish or use flowery language; they do not use terms of endearment or stroke your ego; and they do not speak just to speak. They purposely do not use aphorisms or provide information that is self-evident and already known. They don't sugarcoat! You can recognize them by:

- Their high vibration and energy signature – that is very refined and not readily perceived by the naked eye and can only be discerned by those in Higher-Vibratory states.

- Their demeanor is gentle, loving and without calling attention to themselves. They do not use any fluff.

- They do not use words to speak. They communicate telepathically and through packets of information, pictograms or downloads.

- Their communication is not embellished. It is clear, concise and straight to the point.

- They are no-nonsense and sometimes come across as stern, especially if one of them is working directly with you.

- When they wish to communicate with you, they will and it's not a big production.

- They are meek and humble and usually ask how they can be of service to you.

- When in their presence, the love is so overwhelming that we have nothing on this plane of existence that compares to it. Those in the Truth Movement speak of a fake love induced by Alien technology. One who is already of Higher Consciousness and vibration, and who exercises Discernment, will know the difference.

- If they choose to appear in your presence, they will lower their vibration sufficiently so that you can perceive them with your third eye or inner awareness. Your vibration would have to be high enough to be able to capture the refined vibrational field.

- They do not announce themselves as Master so-and-so or Archangel so-and-so. If you are of a Higher Vibration, you will recognize them readily. If you've worked with any of them in the Higher Realms, you will "Know" their energy signature.

- They do not waste a communication or communicate something that doesn't need to be expressed. They do not waste time on trivial matters or concerns.

- When providing information to you, it is done so on a "need-to-know" basis and only if it serves your Highest Good and according to what you can safely handle at the time, so that it will not impede with your spiritual path or spiritual growth.

- They do not infringe on your free will.

- They serve The Highest Light, which is that of Prime Creator and All Creation, and they serve humanity.

- They are aware of all transgressions against the Plan of Prime Creator and are vigilant, providing guidance and intervention when absolutely necessary. They do not interfere with Earth-based situations or drama, as it is up to us to manifest the Plan of Supreme Creator on this plane of existence. And this is our job, not theirs.

You may be of the opinion that if you can't see them, communicate with them, be heard by them or be helped by them that they don't exist or that they are part of the fallen or Dark Forces. I say that those of us who have this posture may not have the vibration necessary to perceive them or receive their telepathic communication. There are many who have been severely compromised by the Dark Forces with illnesses, trauma, personality disorders, self-esteem issues, victimization issues, interpersonal relationship fiascos, financial challenges and other life drama. So, if you're experiencing any of these, your vibration is at its lowest. The only Beings we can communicate with, under those circumstances, are those that exist in those lower-vibratory states.

THE LOW VIBRATION CYCLE

The Dark Forces implement a Positive Feedback Loop System. Positive, in this case, is not a good thing; instead, it indicates a favorable gain or gain in magnitude for that which instigates the action or behaviors. For example, the Dark Forces create situations that lower your vibration so that they can keep messing with you. As they keep messing with you, you further lower your vibration and then they can access you better in order to mess with you again. This system self-generates the perfect situations or scenarios that, in turn, lead to continuous lower vibration. The purpose of this is that they use your negative energy as food or fuel and keep you from reaching your highest potential.

Let's say you're on your lunch break at work. You get a bite to eat at a local diner, and when you're done, you go to your car and can't find your keys. You realize you left them in the ignition, and you've locked the car. You're upset because now you'll be late to work

– you've been reprimanded about this before. You start cursing in anger. Your vibration is lowered because of your choice to react in a negative fashion. You begin to emit negative energy, which have the astral creatures, entities and parasites taking out their straws and having themselves an afternoon snack. Because they have fed off you, you're now energetically weakened, or more vulnerable. So, they hit you again with another situation where you will not be able to hold your composure, or refrain from emitting negative emotions.

You happen to call AAA so that they can retrieve your keys. When you make the call, the agent on the phone tells you that your AAA membership is expired, and it'll cost you $100 to renew for a whole year. If you don't renew, it will be $100 to get someone out there and open up the door. You don't have that kind of money right now. You are now livid. You emit a greater amount of negative energy, and your vibration goes down even more. They are now wiping their mouths with their bibs, as more of them arrive at the "loosh bar" for their fix. You now call your sister and ask her for the $100 to get your keys out of the car. Your sister is not sympathetic because you haven't paid her back from the last time you did something stupid. She is sarcastic on the phone. Because you are now weakened by the recent negative-emotion-burst, you have reached zero-tolerance and her sarcasm and aloofness sets you off in an emotional tailspin.

You are now even weaker than before. You yell at her and curse her out for being so callous. You are now producing excessive levels of negative energy – again lowering your vibration even further. The entities have just started the grill, getting ready for their tailgate party. This account sounds like just a story to help clarify this concept, but, unfortunately, this is precisely how these entities work. It's a positive feedback loop because the Dark Forces create an action or an aggravating situation that elicits a behavior from you, and each time it benefits the Dark Forces. We provide food for these entities every time we react with a negative emotion, or an adverse reaction tops the one before. On top of that, we become less objective when dealing with other detrimental situations and less resistant to other negative outbursts. And this keeps the cycle going.

The point in all this is that we can't communicate with the Higher-Vibratory Realms without first raising our vibrations – a task that is almost impossible to achieve without understanding 1) the dynamics of what is transpiring and 2) what must be done to break the cycle of this positive feedback loop. (See figure 3)

Positive Feedback Loop System

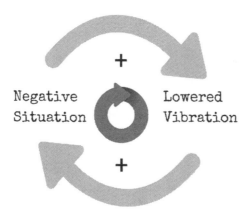

Figure 3

So, to recap, the Truth Movement is a movement that appeals to all those that have moved on from the New Age deceit, but who are still not exercising their discernment-muscles to the fullest. The Dark Forces use the new recruits to disseminate deceitful information to others. They incriminate themselves and then incriminate the Light Forces in order to implicate them in their sinister agenda. It works like a charm!

The Dark Forces are masters of spinning information in order to plant the seeds of doubt. Those of us who serve The Light, but who are not connecting directly with Source-Creator and experiencing high vibration and Higher Truth will share in this doubt and become suspicious of everything. In turn, a witch-hunt ensues that condemns everything that is legitimately of The Light and serving Prime Creator. Thus, we begin to aid the Dark Forces, inadvertently, by holding on to these erroneous notions about the True Beings of Light. Indeed, we are doing a good job at spreading the disinformation – without hesitation, without questioning and with great determination. Finally, they send us on a witch hunt of all the True Beings of Light, thereby keeping us from seeking their guidance and protection, and keeping us from attaining our liberation from this Matrix.

CHAPTER 11

FALSE SPIRITUALITY

~ Mathew 7 ~

15- *"Watch out for false prophets. They come to you in sheep's clothing, but inwardly they are ferocious wolves. 16- By their fruit you will recognize them. Do people pick grapes from thornbushes, or figs from thistles? 17- Likewise, every good tree bears good fruit, but a bad tree bears bad fruit. 18- A good tree cannot bear bad fruit, and a bad tree cannot bear good fruit. 19- Every tree that does not bear good fruit is cut down and thrown into the fire. 20- Thus, by their fruit you will recognize them.*

~ John 4:1~

"Dear Friends, believe not every spirit, but try the spirits whether they are of God: because many false prophets are gone out into the world."

~ Jeremiah 23:16 ~

"This is what the LORD Almighty says: "Do not listen to what the prophets are prophesying to you; they fill you with false hopes. They speak visions from their own minds, not from the mouth of the LORD."

Though the words above were written thousands of years ago, they describe our here and now. We are living in the times described in ancient spiritual texts. Even those who have completely discarded their warning cannot deny that many of the signs predicted in them are very evident today. Whoever wrote these scriptures clearly knew something about what we were going to face.

We'd have to be blind not to see what is transpiring in the world. Much of what was predicted is manifesting as we speak, particularly the plethora of false prophets. There are so many teachers and different ideologies that we don't know what's what anymore. And there is reason to believe that something deceitful, not pure, not coming from The Light of God/Prime Creator is orchestrating this, and nothing is stopping it. Organized religion has been used for centuries as a vehicle to spread many untruths and as a tool to control the masses; however, this section will focus on False Spirituality, because this "new and improved" form of religion is claiming to be the answer for the disheartened.

False spiritual teachers and leaders are those who knowingly or unknowingly teach and/or promote False Spirituality. And, whether they are aware of it or not, they are doing this on behalf of the Dark Forces. These people have enough information about spiritual concepts to make them dangerous to the unaware and non-discerning. They possess charismatic personalities and leadership qualities that make them perfect candidates to be infiltrated, especially if they are not of Higher Consciousness and are a bit unscrupulous. In other words, most don't practice what they preach.

Because many have above average spiritual understandings, they feel they can teach what they think they know, guess on what they don't, and disseminate the information to those willing to receive it. Sometimes the information lacks substance, as it is too general, vague and contrived. Sometimes they'll quote directly from the Bible or other religious text and misinterpret the scripture or message; or, they feel it doesn't apply to them – because they are above that. They have the "walking-on-water" syndrome.

Amazingly, most of their followers don't notice the discrepancies in their teachings, or they don't care. They are too mesmerized by the so-called spiritual teacher's charm, their method of delivery, their charisma, their dominion of language and ability to command respect, and their perceived spiritual attainment. The bottom line is, most followers or students believe that the spiritual teacher or leader has a level of knowledge more advanced than their own.

Sometimes these false prophets will lure a potential student or follower by wowing them with experiential phenomena (or miracles). These experiences may be real or fabricated, but the student does not bother to find out. He or she is attracted to the possibility of finally having an encounter with the Higher Realms or Kingdom of God, and feels that the so-called teacher or leader will be the one to help him achieve this. The student believes – or has been convinced – that they cannot make such a connection on their own.

These false teachers will use their limited knowledge (or take information that is general knowledge and repackage it), adding embellishments and ornamentation to make it sound like it's their Higher Knowledge based on their attainment. To those that don't know any better, it sounds fantastic. The problem is that the student/follower often spends a lot of time studying the teacher's "method", and little to no time developing their own discernment skills. They become dependent on the teacher because the one thing the teacher *doesn't* provide instruction on is how they can connect directly to God or Source and get the information themselves. This empowerment lesson is withheld, either because the teacher wants to keep students dependent or because he is not connecting directly to Source himself.

This section is not meant to dissuade anyone from seeking a genuine teacher or spiritual leader – a teacher that is indeed knowledgeable about and experienced with the Higher Teachings. Higher Teachings is the body of spiritual knowledge and understandings that incorporate the Laws and Protocols of The Higher-Vibratory Realms of Prime Creator, also known as The Kingdom of God. These "real" teachers and spiritual leaders are on the planet right now – but they have to be sought out. The reason is because, as real teachers, they do not shout their "Mastery" from the rooftops. They don't just talk the talk – they walk the walk and are humble, meek and live a life in service-to-others. It is said "when the student is ready, the teacher appears..." You will be led to the right one when your willingness to further your spiritual awakening burns within you, when you need spiritual Truth more than you need to breathe.

One of the most critical takeaways from this book is an awareness of the "over-abundance" of false prophets and false information. When you feel that yearning to grow spiritually, it is imperative that you exercise maximum discernment, for you may have a difficult time with unmasking the imposters from the genuine teachers without it. Unfortunately, this presents somewhat of a catch-22 because when you first begin the journey your discernment skills are the shakiest. Just remember that the surest way to spot a fake teacher is one who doesn't lead by example.

RED FLAGS

Ego

Be very mindful of those that use all sorts of accolades and titles before their names. Others may call them by such titles, but when they address themselves as such, it is a sign of arrogance, or they are trying to "wow" you.

Questionable Behavior

Be mindful of those who claim to have achieved their Spiritual Mastery yet are conducting themselves in ways representative of the Lower-Vibratory Realms. Having addictions of any sort would be a good example of this, as is lying, being manipulative, controlling or conniving. Remember that real representatives of the Higher Octaves or Realms in service to Prime Creator are in a Higher-Vibratory rate due to their impeccable conduct and demeanor, one that is in alignment with the Heart and Mind of the Supreme God. Look at it this way – if your so-called teacher is behaving in a way that is shunned in this Lower-Realm, then they cannot claim to be a teacher of the Light or Higher Truths. If they're not putting their money where their mouth is, you may want to find another teacher.

Holding Back Information

Watch for teachers that dole out bits of information piecemeal, for they are dangling the proverbial carrot in front of your face. Some hold back information on purpose, drawing out each lesson in order to extend their classes or workshops. This information is often very general and is presented as if it's some big overwhelming mystery, something the student cannot understand unless he or she completes numerous levels of training. It is designed to disempower the student and keep them coming back for more information.

There are exceptions to this, of course, for example, the student who indeed needs to learn how to crawl before they can walk, and eventually run. He or she will legitimately enter the lessons as a beginner and gradually move up the rungs of the knowledge ladder. However, to keep a student perpetually at the same or introductory level, despite the fact that he may have grasped the knowledge and mastered it, may indicate that 1) the teacher hasn't mastered any level beyond that or, 2) the teacher doesn't want to empower the student.

Excessive Meditation

Take note of those who speak of reaching states of "nirvana" or being blissed-out without having done the inner spiritual work. Many of these pseudo-spiritual teachers will get the students or followers to go into prolonged periods of meditation for several hours – sometimes even entire days – in order to reach these pseudo-states of bliss. Since many students are seeking to experience these Higher Realms right now, they will gladly follow the guidance of the teacher, not understanding that going into these states for prolonged periods negates the body – the physical – which also is needed for our spiritual growth on this plane of existence.

By blissing out, you are no longer participating on this plane and, therefore, are not engaged in making a difference to correct what is not working and raising the consciousness and vibratory level of humanity. The Higher-Vibratory Realms, where the True States of Bliss are experienced, are not where you are at the present moment. If you were meant to be there, you would not have come here to be of service – you would have stayed there, as many of us come from those Illumined Realms before embodying here.

Spiritual Negligence and Irresponsibility

A genuine spiritual teacher or leader does not have the students remain in those states for prolonged periods of time. This instruction is negligent, irresponsible and guiding the student/follower to practice something that is ultimately spiritually detrimental. A real teacher, one that is connected with The Higher Realms, would have a clear understanding of the need for embodiment on this plane of existence. The spiritual teacher/leader should be instructing students that it is imperative for them to be participating fully in this life and taking a stand against the Dark Forces in order to bring the Divine Plan back to this Lower-Vibratory Realm.

For a person who is not spiritually prepared, remaining in a prolonged "state of bliss" creates a state of imbalance in that person. They find themselves wanting to stay in those so-called blissful states perpetually; they wish to escape the physical body and experience the kind of weightless freedom they had prior to embodiment. This desire to not be fully present is disempowering and creates a need to focus on "Self" in order to achieve these states. This blissed-out state is also known as Samadhi.

ON SAMADHI – QUOTES FROM EXPERTS

What is Samadhi?

"There are several kinds. One type [of Samadhi] is when you are meditating. A current passes through the body, you go into [Samadhi], and you forget about your body. There is another type of [Samadhi] that is deeper than the first. The current passes from the backside of your spine and you go into [Samadhi]. That becomes a sort of standard [Samadhi]. Then there is yet another deeper [Samadhi] where the soul comes out of your body and stabilizes about six inches over the head. Then you can get God realization [Sakshatkara]. After some time the soul re-enters the body. There is also a kind of [Samadhi] in meditation in which one gets experiences. One gets a lot of happiness and forgets about one's body. That is another kind of [Samadhi] that results from the experiences."

—Shiva Bala Yogi

"The stage of perfection is called trance, or [Samadhi], when one's mind is completely restrained from material mental activities by practice of yoga. This is characterized by one's ability to see the self by the pure mind and to relish and rejoice in the self. In that joyous state, one is situated in boundless transcendental happiness and enjoys himself through transcendental senses. Established thus, one never departs from the truth and upon gaining this he thinks there is no greater gain. Being situated in such a position, one is never shaken, even in the midst of greatest difficulty. This indeed is actual freedom from all miseries arising from material contact."

—Bhagavad-Gita 6.20-23

"Samadhi is the highest state of consciousness attainable by men and women. Although many yogis claim to have achieved it, genuine Samadhi is an extremely rare phenomenon. Among the more perfect cases are those described in the principal Upanishads, the inner or mystic revelations that constitute the core teachings of Vedanta. Nowadays, however, the Samadhi attained is almost always only a self-induced hypnotic trance or a swoon-like state of which little or nothing can be remembered when the person returns to the normal state."

—**Gene Kieffer, based on the writings of Pandit Gopi Krishna**

The Dangers of Samadhi

"Sooner or later a meditator will experience [Samadhi], which is a time of rejoicing, and a time for concern. Meditative absorption, as coveted as it may be, is not the point of the path, for we are not trying to create a state of mind that we then label as "spiritual". The point is to be receptive to any state of mind, even those we deem unspiritual. Because our normal mind is so frantic, the experience of [Samadhi] is easily mistaken for a grand realization. The contrast is so dramatic we think [Samadhi] is it."

—**"The Danger of Samadhi", By Andrew Holecek**

"There are three classic meditation experiences waiting to snare the more evolved, or lucky, meditator. They get us because they feel so good. These are the experiences of bliss, clarity, and non-thought, the by-products of meditative absorption. They are the purest honey covering the sharpest hooks. Traleg Rinpoche nails the problem when he says, "The main cause of misperceptions regarding meditation experience is that, after the loss of the initial fervor, we may forget to focus on the essence of meditation and its purpose and instead place more and more emphasis on the underlying meditative experience itself."

— "The Danger of Samadhi", By Andrew Holecek

"Bliss, clarity, and non-thought are delicious states of mind, and they are partial experiences of enlightenment. Bliss is the experience of everything and every thought as heavenly. We delight in whatever occurs. We may feel like we have transcended all conflicting emotions, and express our rapture through song and dance. Bliss easily trips us into believing we have soared into the highest states of realization."

— "The Danger of Samadhi", By Andrew Holecek

According to Enoch, in *The Book of Knowledge: The Keys of Enoch* by Dr. J.J. Hurtak, Samadhi is a "false sense of enlightenment" and creates a state of illusion that can be obtained in low-vibratory planes of existence like planet Earth. Most who achieve this state believe that no further spiritual evolution or soul growth is needed because they have reached the ultimate state of consciousness. They believe that Samadhi is the end-all. They mistakenly believe that they've achieved their way back to Prime Creator, and there is no more spiritual work to be done.

Again, anything that denies or numbs the physical experience takes away from our ability to use our physicality for our spiritual growth, and as a means to help others achieve the same. It is in experiencing our life fully in this density, and by making the right choices, that we expand our consciousness and achieve Self-Mastery.

AGENDA OF THE DARK FORCES AND FALSE SPIRITUALITY

If you strive to have a Higher Consciousness and serve The Light of Prime Creator and all Its Creations, then it's time to awaken from the stupor imposed by the stealthy, nefarious ones. It is time to realize what has been done to most of us via all these pseudo-spiritual campaigns and religions that "hook" us via their sweet-sounding words and luring wisdom. These false concepts and belief systems are meant to perform a "spiritual lobotomy" – a disconnection from the True God or Source/Prime Creator. They also lull us into a false sense of comfort that, of course, leads to spiritual laziness. It keeps us from understanding our role in helping to correct that which is not in alignment – the mess that we've allowed to pile up while we've been self-absorbed and pretending everything was going according to plan.

False Spirituality is like a drug. Imagine if you will someone who is approached by a drug-dealer. This person wouldn't ordinarily engage in conversation with a drug-dealer; except that this time, he's having a rough time with his life and is about to have a nervous breakdown. He asks the drug-dealer if he has something that can take off "the edge". The dealer says, of course, he has the perfect pill. The person takes the drug, and indeed it takes away the anxiety, stress, and bottled-up anger. Now he feels great.

A couple of days later, "the edge" has returned. The person approaches the drug supplier for some more, which the dealer happily produces. The edge disappears again, but it soon comes back and stronger than before. Now the person needs more of this drug to drive this feeling away. The person becomes dependent on this drug-dealer and the pill for their "feel-good" state. They don't realize that while in this state, their house isn't being taken care of, their bills aren't paid on time, and their duties at work are being neglected – because they haven't been fully present. Their feel-good state is becoming detrimental to their wellbeing.

False Spirituality uses pseudo-spiritual teachers and leaders to provide us with beautiful "feel-good" concepts and generalized "truths" to fill the void in our souls. It acts like a drug – like opium. It also provides erroneous answers to our questions that ultimately lead to disempowerment and a state of complacency and inertia. Because we want to be in this feel-good space, we are more likely to push away any information that might spoil it. So, if the Highest Truth were to be revealed to us, Truth that calls upon us to take responsibility for our lives and the adverse conditions in the world, we immediately look the other way. If this Truth shows us that there is an Opponent that we need to be vigilant of, we quickly dismiss it. If this Truth warns us that we need to be more careful about the choices we make when faced with unfavorable situations, so that we don't lower our vibration and find ourselves aiding and abetting the Dark Forces, we swiftly discard it.

We push back against the Truth because we have the numbing effect of the spiritual lies running through our veins. These lies act as a powerful inhibitor, preventing us from enforcing our ability to discern and connect with our Divinity. The spiritual lie has a built-in stop-loss that prevents you from kicking the habit. Our innate desire to get fooled, to know "a truth", regardless of whether it's a lie, activates the "addiction-molecule" within the spiritual-lie-pill. So, if we allow the Real Truth in, it will bring us down from our pseudo-spiritual high, and we will fight this with every ounce of our being. We rationalize that if it "feels good", then it must be true, and we don't realize that we have become addicted. False Spirituality has become like our opium – our drug of choice – compliments of the deception-pushers, working for the Dark Forces. Subconsciously, we know that the Real Truth cuts like a knife, and this is painful – and sometimes, we avoid it at all cost.

The Real Truth is that "The Truth" is within you. It has been all along. There is no need to seek it from compromised, outside sources. You don't need to numb yourself with overly-decorated Truisms, or escape the physical world by blissing out in order to get closer to it. What you must do, however, is summon the courage to face "The Truth", regardless of how uncomfortable it makes you feel. And once you are face-to-face with it, you do need to have the willingness to act on it.

Again, you are a Spark from The Divine Creator and have the Divine Components within you. Because this is so, you have the Divine Power and Divine Authority to eradicate evil and darkness – *all* evil and *all* darkness from this realm! It doesn't happen automatically. You have to be cognizant of who you are, what the Plan of Creator is and what your role is. You also have to be open to accepting your role within the *Grand Plan* and then propel yourself into *action*! If you're too busy getting duped and being in those states of complacency and indifference, you not only fail as an individual, but you also fail the entire human race and all the life-forms expressing on the planet.

Right now you might be asking, how is all this my responsibility? It's not just yours. It falls on all of us. However, if we each take the posture of "it's not my job" or "it's not my responsibility", we all fail! So, it boils down to each one of us, individually, taking the responsibility to take action! We've come in as Divine Emissaries, Ambassadors, and Spiritual, Light Warriors to bring all life on the planet back into alignment with the Will of God. It happens on our watch, and the moment is now. It's time to break the addiction!

CHAPTER 12

CHANNELED MESSAGES & ASTRAL ENTITIES

"The whole secret lies in confusing the enemy, so that he cannot fathom our real intent."

"So in war, the way is to avoid what is strong, and strike at what is weak."

"Those skilled at making the enemy move do so by creating a situation to which he must conform; they entice him with something he is certain to take, and with lures of ostensible profit they await him in strength."

"Hence to fight and conquer in all your battles is not supreme excellence; supreme excellence consists in breaking the enemy's resistance without fighting."

"…mystify, mislead, and surprise the enemy"

—Sun Tzu, "The Art of War"

Channeled information comprises most of what is considered New Age spiritual information today. Anyone who wants to get clarity on a subject having to do with spirituality, the Ascension, or with respect to the End of the Great Cycle or ETs, is being bombarded by a slew of books, blogs, articles and videos of "chan-neled" material. Every day, there is someone else who claims to channel a well-known Master or ET group, or Off-World Coun-cil. Most of the messages, again, blend in truths, intermixed with bits of untruths that are so artfully placed that they go unnoticed. The messenger is so convincing – having already earned trust – that the disinformation is immediately embraced and incorporated into one's belief system.

Now, there are those who channel "Higher Knowledge"; how-ever, I don't label this as channeling. The term I use is "transmission". When I receive information from Prime Creator or Higher-Vibra-tory Beings in service to Prime Creator, this information is in the form of a download or a "transmission" of information. The body isn't taken over by some entity, personality or other consciousness. I receive packets of information or pictograms, and then I have to find the language to be able to communicate the information, language that precisely conveys the message. So, the process is much different from what I label as channeling.

The channeled material that is discussed in this chapter is of the deceptive kind. Channeling is not a communication method used by High-Vibratory Beings or the Light Forces. It is, however, a favor-ite method used by the Dark Forces, as they disguise themselves as benign, Beings of the Higher Realms, in order to propagate the lies. These lies are specifically targeted for the unaware, and the non-Dis-cerning, who then in turn create websites and blog sites that dissem-inate the so-called "channeled teachings" to the rest of us. People then comment on the blog posts or articles, etc., which inspire even more posts, and thus, the channeled information is spread as if it were the "new gospel".

If you come across information that sounds authentic because it is presented in a loving manner, with beautiful words that seem like they're coming from an Illumined Being, but do not reflect what you are currently witnessing in the outer world, have the courage to walk away from it. If there is one grain of untruth, it is a deceptive message with an agenda. No Truth that comes from Source-Creator will ever be obscured or cloaked or have parts that are Truth and parts that are not. Truth is not part-time or a lunch portion! It is complete and whole. Furthermore, the Truth will not be Truth if it is used to deceive or manipulate. There is no agenda with Truth. It stands alone. It is naked. It needs no qualifying. It is pristine and crystal clear.

The Truth is Truth because it comes from The Light – from Source. There are no shadows or gray areas. It is Light. It rings true with the utterance of the first word of a message, all the way through to the last word. It is transparent; it vibrates with the frequencies of Supreme Creator and all those that serve The Light.

Remember that these entities mimic what we believe is the speech and phraseology of the True Light Beings. When you hear a channeled message from a so-called Ascended Master, you will notice that information is adorned with flowery words, many terms of endearment and much sugar-coating of the subject matter. Everything in the world seems to be in order, on track, and everything is as it should be. The so-called Master-Imposter that is speaking claims that he has things under control or that the Host of Heaven is taking care of it. Sometimes dates are given, so as to keep you engaged, excited and holding on to the false promise. The prize for the entities creating this illusion is the "let-down" because with the "let-down" comes disappointment, jadedness, cynicism and a slew of other lower-vibratory emotions.

In the Higher-Vibratory Realms, the Beings of Light are not involved with the everyday realities of this world. That is for all of us to take care of through our direct involvement. The messages that claim everything is alright and being taken care of aim to disempower you, make you indifferent, over-confident, complacent, disengaged and apathetic. As a consequence, you stop wanting to help correct what's not working in this world, since the *Beings of Light* will swoop down and turn things around – so you're led to believe. And this is a blatant lie. Only we, working together, can turn it around. It is only us, stepping into our Divine Power and Divine Authority, which will raise the consciousness and vibration of humanity to the highest level possible.

The Beings in service to The Light are busy. They are busy "taking care of business" and most of that business doesn't pertain to this plane of existence. They are also fully engaged in taking care of that which can only be taken care of by Beings that have attained a very high level of consciousness or Christ/God-Consciousness. On Earth, due to the low-vibratory level and a third-dimensional density, only we can handle the situations here. We do so using our physicality, for it takes a body to be able to effect the changes necessary.

Why would you be in embodiment and then choose not to take responsibility for all that embodiment entails? What causes this "It's not my problem" or "It's all being taken care of" thought process? If you have already achieved Mastery before embodiment and come in having an understanding of your role in this world, isn't it a bit suspicious that you would think in this manner? Four things could cause this way of thinking: 1) you are still veiled and don't remember who you truly are, 2) you remember who you are and you "choose" to pass the buck on the responsibility part, 3) you are royally being messed with by the Dark Forces who have fed you disinformation and 4) you've fully incorporated the new software program that the Sinister Forces wrote to override your Original and Divine Blueprint. The purpose of this book is to break you out of whatever spell you're under or whatever "software program" has taken over you. The understanding of the concepts presented will hopefully lead you to making the kind of choices that empower you, as opposed to those that disempower.

You need to take advantage of every moment that you are alive, in order to use your physical body to help implement change at every level – the physical, mental, emotional and spiritual. This change is not just a personal one, but one that affects the world at large. This change happens when you're *fully participating* in life, making the appropriate choices and taking appropriate action. This means that you've been born into a realm like this one to take advantage of every opportunity to be of service by being "a voice"for those who can't speak for themselves, by building harmonious societies, by planting a garden, by motivating and empowering, by marching for a cause, by consoling an elderly person or a child, and being the role models for the New, High-Vibrational Earth.

If you believe the storyline laid out for you in this reality, you will soon forget that you are truly a Master of Light. And when you do forget, you will listen to messages that are not coming from the Highest Truth and Light of the Supreme Creator – instead, these will be low-vibratory messages from the representatives of the Lower Realms. Why would you consciously connect with anything other than Source-Creator?

These false ones, especially the entities that come in through channelers, are impersonators who have mastered the art of regurgitating words that sound pleasant to the ear of those that cannot discern, cannot remember who they are, or choose not to remember because it would mean they are accountable. Many who have this self-imposed amnesia have become groupies of certain channelers. You can probably name several folks who've made names for themselves through channeling. Some of these famous channelers have created a cult. And when you're in one of these cults, it is hard to discern.

These cult leaders convolute the truth to serve their personal agenda or the agenda of the Dark Forces that animates them. The members have been severely compromised, becoming dependent on the information presented like a junkie needing his next fix. How does one break free from this hypnosis, this trance? It is very difficult. It takes someone with a lot of willpower and courage to break free from this, and someone who can realize that they have given their power away – and the keys to their soul – to deceptive entities.

If you are compromised in this manner, coming to the realization that you're dependent on others for spiritual guidance and Truth is very difficult, thanks to the onslaught of feel-good messages and peer pressure. But if you don't shake off the trance, you become a disinformation agent yourself, working for the Dark Forces and helping to maintain the dark and negative conditions that are currently manifesting on the planet.

DEPENDENCY ON TRIVIALITY

There is a lot of channeled information that discusses the history of mankind, the origins of this planet and solar system, and how humanity has been genetically manipulated by off-world intelligence. Although entertaining and educational, it is not the kind of information that would come from a source representing the Higher Realms. In the grand scheme of things, this type of information is trivial. It is there to quench the mind, to feed the "need to know". It doesn't help raise your vibration or achieve your Self-Mastery. Instead, it is meant to "wow" you and to make you trust the source of the information because, after all, we all want to know our origins. And those that can provide this insight tend to gain our trust.

Real Beings of Light, in service to Prime Creator, will only provide information that edifies you and instructs you on how to tap into your divinity so that you are empowered and can get closer to Source-Creator on your own. Any message that is not providing you with the inspiration or instruction on how to transcend limitations via Self-Mastery or connect directly to Source-Creator is just information to keep you entertained – intrinsically, it achieves nothing for you.

When you don't connect directly with Source, you will more readily embrace information that provides clarity about your existence and your personal predicament. You receive "false clarity", graciously accepting and incorporating it as part of your spiritual regimen and understanding. This type of information will sometimes take you down an entirely different path – or rabbit hole – that you may not have "signed up for". When you trust a channeler or "messenger" implicitly because their messages have made you feel good in the past, it is very hard to discern that the information given is not complete Truth. Furthermore, you may not be able to detect that the message is not originating from a Being of Light in service to Source/Prime Creator.

Dependence on this type of communication is a tough habit to kick. You have been steered away from The Great Light of Supreme Creator; thus, you cannot recognize the True Light because you've become desensitized to the sublime and refined frequencies that require complete focus, discernment and "at-one-ment". By entertaining channeled information, you make a choice as to which "radio station" you want to listen to. When you listen to a particular station or "channel", you'll get a lower-frequency that provides very distinct, "canned" information created specifically to quench the need for knowledge, to keep your mind occupied. In order to tune into the Illumined Information, you have to fine-tune your instrument of reception – yourself – and become more spiritually refined by raising your frequency to match that of those Higher Realms.

Usually, if something is in the gray area with respect to accuracy or vibration, it is *not* coming from The Light. It has more than likely been manipulated to feed your need to know. Channeled beings claiming to be Ascended Masters, Angels and such are really Lower-Dimensional Entities whose knowledge and information is limited to that of the Astral Realm. These provide information that seems spiritually and technologically sound and more advanced. They are deceptive and use these tactics to mislead for self-gratification and adoration. These entities are in service to self and in service to the powers and principalities that govern the Lower-Frequency-Realms. They come across as wise, eloquent, benign beings displaying Spiritual Mastery, but this is just a front to get you to lower your guard and make you trust them implicitly.

A Better Source of Information

I ask you: "What do you say?" "What do you know?" Why are you so dependent on others for your answers?" Shouldn't we all be in the Age of Enlightenment by now? What is causing us to return to the Middle Ages, to a pseudo-spiritual practice that enslaves rather than frees us? Is this a "New Age" of spiritual slavery, one of spiritual arrogance and delusion, an age manufactured by the Dark Forces – Forces that many of us negate? Is this Atlantis all over again? Who or what benefits from us being under this spiritual hypnosis?" I know deep down inside you know the answer to most of these questions by now.

If you want to know Truth, then it is time to remove your sandals, symbolically, and enter humbly into direct communion with Supreme Creator – The All That Is – The One. What force in this Universe would love you more? Which Power would protect you more, or know you more? Wouldn't it make sense to plug directly into the current of Creation, instead of plugging into a AAA battery charger?

By connecting to Source, you can ask all your questions and receive direct and correct answers. No words need to be spoken. Prime Creator and the Beings of Light in service to Prime Creator communicate *directly* with each one of us. We do not need a translator or spiritual broker. Many of us have chosen to tune out; we have changed the channel that receives the Higher Frequencies to that which receives and resonates with the Lower Frequencies. However, now is the time to change it back. It takes work and commitment to wean ourselves from the disinformation being spoon-fed to us, but this is the only way to obtain the Highest Truth.

THE METHOD OF COMMUNICATION FOR BEINGS OF LIGHT

The Higher-Vibrational Beings do not need "channels" to communicate with us. It is all about raising your vibration so that you are on the same frequency. Communication with these Higher-Vibrational Beings does not occur in the fashion you are accustomed to on this plane. It occurs instantaneously, through *whole packets* of information that are downloaded seamlessly, and then unfolds as a *Knowing*. There are no terms of endearment such as "Dear Ones", or "Dear Hearts" or "Beloveds"; words found in our everyday vernacular are also not used. In fact, there is no speech involved at all. The communication is straight and to the point.

Sweet words are often just a lovely package in which to wrap false information. Is there any wonder why "mass landings" or "aerial displays" that have been predicted by channeled messages haven't occurred? How many more failed predictions need to transpire – predictions about contact with ETs, mass arrests of greedy Cabal, Ascension and "Event" dates that haven't happened – for the realization to finally sink in that a lot of this channeled information isn't accurate?

Each and every one of us has the capacity to raise our vibration and have a One-on-One communication with the Higher-Vibratory Beings in Service to Prime Creator, and with Prime Creator directly.

In other words, it doesn't require someone who is deemed to have particular "gifts" or who is more spiritually privileged than others, or who has an "in" with these Beings. It is also not a privilege of those that claim to be ET contactees or those who work with Higher-Vibrational extraterrestrials (known as Ultraterrestrials).

Also, please note that these Beings of Light don't need to prove anything to anyone. The Ultraterrestrials, for example, have no disclosure timeline in place, and they don't need to show themselves openly in our skies. They have no intention of participating in "mass landings" and they do not provide unnecessary or deceptive information. Along those lines, the True Ascended Masters do not involve themselves with triviality or divulge information that has no purpose, or that gives false expectations. Their messages are not meant to disempower you by making you complacent and apathetic. Any information that specifies dates; that is fluffed-up or embellished; that contains terms of endearment; that provides false hope; that gives information that is incongruent with what is being witnessed in the outside world, by telling you that everything is fine and being taken care of, is infiltrated by the Dark Forces for the purpose of 1) disempowering you, 2) giving you false hope and 3) furthering their agenda.

It is up to you, especially now that you are informed, to not fall for their trickery. You do this by going within, anchoring in your heart and connecting to Source-Creator. Every other type of Earth-based connection through leaders, teachers, gurus, etc., or contact with entities of the Astral Realm or Lower-Vibrational ETs, will provide you with disinformation, massive distortions of Truth and lies. Communication and messages from sources other than Prime Creator or Higher-Vibratory Beings in service to Prime Creator will keep you in a stupor and docile – a huge advantage for the Opponent to gain more territory and strength.

IMPOSTOR-ENTITY COMMUNICATION HIGHLIGHTS

Again, channeled information is like a "drug" the spiritually hungry get addicted to. On some level, the user knows the "drug" is harmful but believes he is impervious to such harm. And just like any drug people take in order to help them function, channeled information is used to help many of us function. We think it gives us clarity and direction – even a purpose! We assume that we are spiritually strong and spiritually mature enough to hear these messages and separate the good information from the disinformation. If this is so, then I say that we are spiritually strong and mature enough to connect directly with the All-Knowing, The Light of Prime Creator, and tap into that *uncorrupted Information* directly from the Source of All Information! Get rid of the "Disinformation Brokers"... and yes, I'm coining this term!

Here are some examples of the Red Flags to be looking out for when listening to or reading channeled information. Please note that you may encounter a combination of what is presented. But, rest assured that the True Beings of Light or Ascended Masters and Higher-Vibratory extraterrestrials known as Ultraterrestrials, do not embellish, use terms of endearment or words that are found in our everyday vernacular. And their method of communication is telepathic.

1) **Terms of Endearment**
   - Dear Ones
   - Dear Hearts, Blessed Hearts
   - Beloveds, My Beloved Ones
   - Precious Hearts, My Precious Hearts

2) **Introduction or Announcement of themselves**
   - I am Lord St. Germain
   - This is Archangel Michael
   - This is Ascended Master El Morya
   - This is the Solar Logos
   - I am Lord Metatron

3) **Speak trivialities and generalities**
   - The Forces of Darkness are very active
   - The Light Forces are very busy
   - There is much suffering
   - There is no time to waste
   - The time is at hand

4) **Provide spiritual Truisms** – They provide us with information that is already out there, providing no new insights. The Dark Forces will use commonly accepted facts, especially spiritual understandings that are known to most; they adorn them with flowery speech and present these to you in a beautiful, gift box so that you take them in as if new. Then, once you agree that what is said is true – because your soul recognizes the Truisms – you lower your guard down and also take in the nuggets of disinformation.

5) **Fluff and Embellishments** – This is a puffing up of the information to make it sound grandiose or more than it really is. The information is usually laced with colorful adjectives associated with the message to make it seem that a Master or Higher-Being is speaking from an Illumined Realm. The message is sugary and syrup-coated to make it more appealing and more palatable. Beautiful words and expressions adorn the speech or written material. Embellishments are used to make a fictitious statement sound authentic. It's all window dressing.

6) **Falsities and Lies**

    a. **Everything is alright** – If you are half awake and are honest with yourself, you will see that everything is not alright and that there are many on this planet, including other life here, that are suffering and have no say so as to what is being done to them.

    b. **Everything is in Divine Order** – Everything is not in "Divine Order" since what is currently manifesting on this plane of existence is a hijacking and an aberration of the Original Blueprint of Prime Creator. Suffering and extermination of life-forms is not in Divine Order.

    c. **The Forces of Light are taking care of it** – The Forces of Light are taking care of what they take care of – that which requires their Higher Vibration and specialty. Everything that is in this Lower-Vibratory Realm is the responsibility of the Light Emissaries, otherwise known as the Light Ground-Crew – us. Yes, the Beings of Light in Service to Prime Creator do provide assistance, but it isn't part of the Protocol of The Higher Realms for them to interfere; and it isn't their responsibility to turn things around for us, because we failed due to our choices and disconnection to Source. Turning things around, in order to re-establish the Original Blueprint, is one of the main reasons we are here.

    d. **All the Dark Forces, Entities, Demons, Negative ETs have been taken off the planet** – This notion that the Dark Forces and their minions have been removed from the world is disinformation. You only have to turn on the T.V. or go online to see the global atrocities occurring each and every day, to see the Dark Forces at work. They want nothing more than for you to think they aren't here and that you don't have to focus on them or worry about them anymore. Then, when you go about your "merry way", they have full reign and go unchecked.

e. **Mass arrests will be forthcoming** – The ones predicted haven't occurred, and to say they are forthcoming is a Truism.

   If we all take a stand, grow some backbone and take action, mass arrests and mass corrections will happen. But the promise that this is going to be done for us via an external, Off-World Force is the disinformation.

f. **Everyone will go to Fifth-Dimensional Earth** – Not everyone's vibration will be a match for fifth-dimensional frequencies. Some may go to even higher dimensions than that, and some may not go anywhere.

g. **There is no more HAARP or negative technologies, the Beings of Light have stopped it** – Up to now, these technologies are still being used and are very much in operation, creating weather manipulation and earthquakes. The Beings of Light haven't meddled in our affairs with respect to governments, black ops and other Sinister Forces in service to the Dark Forces, as this is the realm that we're responsible for.

h. **Radiation has been cleaned up** – Radiation levels are high in the Fukushima area and are showing up as being high on the West Coast of the United States and moving across the North American continent.

These high radiation levels have been measured by independent people on this continent, and the readings are consistent.

i. **Putting our attention to conditions and situations that are transpiring on the planet serves to bring them into your reality or make these more prominent** – This concept is disinformation and a technique used for disempowerment. Not putting your attention on these things helps in the escalation, propagation and continuation of these conditions. And by not being mindful of these circumstances and situations, you are aiding and abetting the Dark Forces that are creating them and keeping them in place.

j. **The bad things that happen to us in this embodiment are due to karma and/or contracts we signed before incarnation** – The Dark Forces tell us, via New Age and other spiritual teachers, texts and channeled information that the reason you suffer is because you contractually agreed to this before you embodied. This is supposed to explain why you keep suffering and lead a miserable life; why you're abused and experience illness and lack; why you're raped, maimed, tortured, lose a loved one and have interpersonal, relationship problems; and why you can't get out of one situation without going into another one. All along, these Sinister, Malevolent Forces are the ones instigating, orchestrating, creating the dark, unconscionable scenarios that create such grief and despair as to make living intolerable. These conditions are set up by servants of the Dark Forces, which feed off of the lower-frequency-emotions emitted by the suffering. This low-vibrational energy that is emitted through the emotions elicited through suffering is known as **loosh**.

7) **Using Speech when communicating** – Higher-Vibrational Beings do not use speech to communicate. Communication occurs via telepathic transmissions also known as downloads, which come in as a pictogram and all at once. It then unfolds into your *Knowing*.

8) **Seeking Worship or Calling Attention to Self** – True Beings of Light in service to Prime Creator do not seek worship and do not need to call attention to themselves. They don't brag about their Mastery, or about who they are or what they've accomplished. Any speech or communication that expresses this type of ego-based spiel is clearly a service-to-self, lower-vibrational entity trying to impress and "wow" those who seek information and guidance from that which is outside themselves.

9) **Preach that all judgment is bad** - The idea of being "in judgment", according to the followers of the New Age Movement and certain other spiritual groups, is a negative thing. They state that judgment leads to separation and separation is a no-no, as we are all trying to be One – especially since we're all One at Source. So there are many from the spiritual community who frown on judging anything or anybody; when someone does, they call that person out as being "in judgment". And there lies the paradox, for stating that someone is in judgment also makes *them* judgmental.

This anti-judgment stance is a tool of the Dark Forces, designed to stop you from figuring out what they're up to (and subsequently taking action to stop them). These Forces create certain ideas and concepts that, through carefully orchestrated campaigns, infiltrate your mind like a virus infiltrates your computer. And like a computer virus, sometimes you don't even realize these "programs" are running in the background, corrupting the system.

Contrary to popular New Age opinion, judgment is a paramount tool in our discernment arsenal. It helps us to separate the stuff that brings us closer to our Divine purpose from the junk that pulls us away from Source. New-Agers, though, will tell us that it is judgment that causes the separation, and as our goal is all about achieving Unity Consciousness, we will steer clear of anything that *appears* to threaten it. So when those who have been compromised by the Dark Forces are displaying behavior that is not in alignment with The Light, we're not supposed to call it out or attempt to correct it – because we'll be "in judgment", which equals separation. The mechanism that prevents the detection and eradication of this "spiritual virus" is ingrained by New Age concepts and then policed by the compromised Light Emissaries themselves!

The Dark Forces have also installed another ingenious mechanism within us – they have taught us to chastise ourselves for getting angry. Although anger is a lower vibration emotion, righteous anger propels us forward, allowing us to take action against situations that are out of balance or unjust. When we see injustice or acts of cruelty, and express righteous anger and seek justice, the representatives of the Dark Forces are right there to say we're not loving, not at peace, not in unity consciousness, unforgiving, intolerant, etc. They are quick to tell us that we're displaying attributes of representatives of Lower-Vibrational Realms. In short, they are accusing us of serving the Dark Forces if we show outrage or take corrective measures. They use this tactic to prevent us from defeating them, for if we do we're just like them. That is very slick, indeed.

So, in order for us not to be like them, and be of The Light, we need to look the other way, stand down, deny the existence of these Forces, and not be mindful of the suffering that is happening on the planet. And like most good New Age practitioners, we should work on our so-called Ascension and not dwell on the negative. In the meantime, these heinous Forces have carte blanche to do as they please with this world and all life on it!

This type of propaganda is what many of us have been embracing, without realizing who is behind the disinformation and why it's being disseminated. We embrace it because we think we need to come disarmed, in peace, turn the other cheek, just send love and light, and all the evil and evildoers will just put down their arms. The Dark Forces will leave gracefully and the planet will raise its vibration, and Ascend along with the entire human race. Again, this is all fantasy. Many of us in the spiritual community have been abiding by those false beliefs for years, and it has not advanced the planet. What we see, instead, is more negativity and more suffering. We see exponential entropy.

Because most of us are Spiritually Evolved Emissaries from other Higher-Vibratory Realms, we are experts in our field; and our purpose is not only to uphold The Light, but to put in place the Will of Creator back into a world that is no longer in balance. We come with our Swords of Truth and Wisdom, and we use these to correct all that needs rectifying. This does not occur by acting like spiritual wimps. We need to be *spiritual lions* and eradicate what is trying to quash the Light and all life on the planet. Embracing spiritual practices that make us stand down and lay down for the slaughter is not what the Spiritual Emissaries' directives are. These erroneous thoughts and understandings have been implanted by the Dark Forces in their tactics to weaken The Forces of Light that are currently in embodiment.

CHAPTER 13

THE DECEPTION SENTINELS

"For my part, whatever anguish of spirit it may cost, I am willing to know the whole truth; to know the worst and to provide for it."

—Patrick Henry

"If your opponent is of choleric temper, seek to irritate him. Pretend to be weak, that he may grow arrogant."

—Sun Tzu, "The Art of War"

Who are the sentinels that keep the system – this Matrix, if you will – in place? Who are the ones making sure that the disinformation campaigns continue their onslaught, and who are the ones diluting the message when some of us speak a truth that threatens to expose the shenanigans of the Dark Forces? Sentinels are deliberately appointed to the task of disseminating the disinformation and countering any information that dispels the propaganda of the Dark Forces. They usually work in groups and are scattered throughout the different avenues of communication and information sources that are available today. These Sentinels guard the disinformation, regardless what type it is: world affairs, political, financial, scientific, environmental and spiritual. Their job is to distribute and safeguard that which keeps the "sleeping" masses, and those that are aware of what's happening behind the scenes, from doing anything about it.

These Sentinels, in human form, work advertently or inadvertently for the Dark Forces, serving as their minions. Some of them know their role and have the tactics and skill-sets of highly trained soldiers. These specialized ones have a very no-nonsense demeanor. They possess a very high level of intelligence and a fine-tuned cunningness that allows them to carry out agendas and put into place strategies that will shoot down attempts to shatter the Matrix.

Then there are those who used to be members of the Light Forces but have been taken over because of weaknesses in character or lowered vibration. The decreased vibration was caused by inappropriate choices in beliefs, emotions, thoughts and actions that have led them down the path of descension, as opposed to Ascension. These folks are the best suited for the task of being a Sentinel since they know many of the members of the light community. They are probably well liked and trusted; they also know the vulnerabilities of this group. These Sentinels can also "talk the talk", which makes it easy for them to disseminate new disinformation packets or keep circulating older ones to the non-discerning members of that community. They do so thinking they are in service of others. They're embraced as a member of the "light community" when – unbeknownst to themselves – they are acting as an agent for the Dark Forces.

How does this work and why is it important to know? These folks are placed in strategic forums, chat groups, websites, social media sites, radio shows – and other venues that disseminate information – for the supposed purpose of sharing "spiritual knowledge" with others. This material is filled with the many Truisms that have been repackaged by the New Age Movement. It is used to shoot down any train of thought or perspective that clearly exposes the strategies of the Dark Forces, strategies that aim to keep the masses and the spiritual groups subdued and dumbed-down.

These Sentinels have a collective or "beehive" mindset – they work together as a team with a common goal. Let's say, for example, that you see a blog post that is attempting to disseminate spiritual disinformation. You leave a comment aiming to expose the blog as New Age propaganda. Shortly after you leave the comment, one of the Sentinels takes the initiative to respond to your comment and in defense of the blog post. Then another Sentinel will stand right behind the first Sentinel as a sign of support, thus giving the illusion of strength. Their goal is to discredit *you* – the person who is trying to expose the true agenda of the Dark Forces. A second and third Sentinel may also pop in to show solidarity. I have termed this tactic "spiritual bullying", and it is carried out by what I call "spiritual gangs."

ATTRIBUTES OF A SPIRITUAL BULLY

If you run across the following personality traits, you are probably dealing with a spiritual bully/Sentinel. Either you step into your power and authority or you might just have to walk away and leave these folks thinking they've won. Walking away will help fuel their delusional problem, unfortunately. Here are the traits:

Arrogance – There is this demeanor of aggrandizement, of spiritual superiority, and of entitlement. They act as if they've attained enlightenment. In truth, no one that has reached any Higher Spiritual Mastery behaves in such a manner. As mentioned before, those that have attained a Higher Consciousness are very humble, quiet and reserved. They walk the walk alone, unannounced and unnoticed.

Enormous Ego – It is clear that the ego hasn't been tamed and is being used as a weapon. Part of the game is to act as if they're more astute than the other person; they always present themselves as an expert. If the other person doesn't understand the infiltrated disinformation, then it is made to seem that the other person doesn't have a grasp of the concept and, therefore, isn't spiritually mature.

Delusion – They have a delusion that they are spiritually accomplished, when their behavior shows otherwise. Other delusions are that the world is doing just fine and that their lives are perfect – because they follow a spiritual regimen, which everyone should also be following. Within their minds is that perfect Utopia and they make believe the world at large matches that image.

Closed to other perspectives – The only acceptable point of view or belief system is their own. It is usually obtained through the New Age Movement and acquired through spiritually immature teachers who were incapable of walking their talk. They've learned how to master the art of regurgitating concepts, using New Age jargon.

Need to correct – They have this intense desire or urge to comment after someone has posted something or written a book that is not along the lines of their belief system – for example, posting a book review or leaving a comment that puts down the author and his or her point of view. They do this in a public manner, making the victim feel as if they are spiritual newbies or spiritually inept. They have a need to correct your information or knowledge.

Self-Imposed Master – Yes, they have knighted themselves into being a Spiritual Master. They would call themselves an Ascended Master, but they know that people will wonder why they still have biological needs. Their behavior is indicative of a person who hasn't yet awakened to a "beginners level" of spirituality.

Demeaning – This is a tactic used by the Dark Forces and their minions to create doubt in the Spiritual Emissary. The goal here is to shake the Emissary's confidence and distrust their Knowing. If they can do this, then they can get them to rely on others for their information and spiritual guidance. As the Spiritual Emissary relies on outside sources, they will receive indoctrination and a whole lot of disinformation to keep them complacent, docile, in a stupor, and disconnected from their Source of Power. Once they're under this "hypnosis", they are not cognizant of the actual agenda of the Dark Forces and their cohorts. And there is no interest to take appropriate action to correct what is not in alignment with the Will of Prime Creator.

Parrot Syndrome – They regurgitate concepts and phrases they've heard from others and then quote them like a pastor would quote passages from the Bible. The little "snippets" become the artillery used in their verbal attacks. Some phrases used are: "this is fear porn"; "you're fear-mongering"; "what you think you bring into your reality"; "you're in separation", and "you're in judgment". These phrases and concepts are used to create doubt in yourself and stop you from developing your train of thought or making your point. It is meant as a way to prevent you from tearing down their delusion or alerting others about the deception.

SPIRITUAL GANGS

What's better than one Spiritual Bully? How about two or more? If several people are berating you and corralling you into a corner, this is a sign that you have encountered a gang or pack. Because they have been severely compromised and their posture is based on fluff and disinformation, there is always another one of these impostors waiting on the sidelines, ready to back up the initial bully and lend credence to what they are saying. They will take turns in responding to someone who has written information, like a blog post, an article or a book, about a topic that exposes the deception. Sometimes they lurk in chat rooms or forums and attack a post or a video that aims at empowering and awakening others from the grip of spiritual bondage. Instead of ignoring something that doesn't pertain to them, they go all out to make an example of the person they're in disagreement with or that aims to shatter the hypnosis posed by the disinformation.

This experience leaves a very sour taste in anyone's mouth – whether you are on the receiving end of the beating or just a spectator. And it's not easy to shake off. It makes you wonder what we're up against because if this bullying behavior is a representation of The Light, we're in major trouble – and we are. The good news is that bullying is not a quality of the Light. The bad news is that it is an indication of the Dark Forces having taken over those that at one time served the Light. This takeover is often very subtle and stealth, and very strategic.

NEGATIVE REINFORCEMENT – PAVLOV'S DOG

It is of utmost importance to discern how these Dark Forces work and how they weave their sinister threads into everything. Awareness of this is key because these Sinister Ones are ingenious and so on top of their game that we will start getting sick when we hear spiritual terms or listen to this type of information. Remember that these Dark Forces know us better than we know ourselves. So, how do they instill a distaste for spirituality so that we become further disconnected from Prime Creator and the Higher-Vibratory Realms? How do they use this tactic to keep us in the Matrix, not allowing us to pursue Self/Spiritual Mastery?

The Dark Forces and their minions not only create discord within the spiritual community, but they also pair up negative feelings with the unpleasant incidents that occur while practicing spirituality. These events usually happen when confrontations occur with Spiritual Bullies. Some of these feelings can range from anger, resentment, embarrassment, self-unworthiness, self-doubt and hate. Because we don't like experiencing these feelings, we begin to avoid the topics that lead to the negative encounters that elicit these emotions. And when we hear the subject matter again, we run the other way, leave a forum, delete the blog or just go on a different path. We stop speaking about or practicing spirituality in order to avoid the negative experiences we've had with it. As a consequence, we also disconnect from Source-Creator, as we associate *It* as also being a part of this equation.

The technique is called Conditioning and was studied in depth by Ivan Pavlov. Pavlov discovered that a dog would salivate when a bowl of food was placed in front of it. When certain stimuli, like a bell, were introduced before the bowl of food was given, the dog learned that when he heard the bell ring, the bowl of food was coming. He would then begin to salivate at the sound of the bell alone, even when the food was not in front of him. This type of conditioning is called positive reinforcement, where a person or animal learns how to behave or react using positive stimuli. You hear the bell, you get the food, and you salivate. Then you hear the sound, and you salivate because you expect the food.

What the Dark Forces have done is present us with a Negative Reinforcement – another way to learn as well. This type of learning occurs when we want to avoid negative stimuli. We acquire new behaviors and attitudes based on avoidance. In order not to experience anger whenever we encounter animosity or discord about spiritual topics with others in forums, chat rooms or social media, we ultimately avoid the subject altogether. We learn to attribute spirituality as being the cause of the unpleasant feelings and emotional pain by what is referred to as Transference. We "transfer" the negative feelings elicited by the "Bullies" in the chat rooms to the subject matter, and we subconsciously blame the subject matter for the negative feelings.

We begin to associate spirituality in general with getting angry, frustrated and stressed which causes us to view anything that is spiritually empowering as a turn-off. This type of conditioning is one of the many ways that the Dark Forces get you to stand down and not become empowered. And we become disempowered when we become disconnected from our source of power – Source-Creator. Being totally aware of these Sentinels – aka Spiritual Bullies – is part of your spiritual awareness-arsenal and will help you avoid the pitfalls when you encounter them.

"*Then you will know the truth, and the truth will set you free.*"

—John 8:32

"*Three things cannot be long hidden: the sun, the moon, and the truth.*"

—Buddha

"*Thousands of candles can be lighted from a single candle, and the life of the candle will not be shortened.*"

—Buddha

Part III

Tipping the Balance in Our Favor

CHAPTER 14

CHALLENGES IN DISCERNMENT

"Bravery without forethought, causes a man to fight blindly and desperately like a mad bull. Such an opponent, must not be encountered with brute force, but may be lured into an ambush and slain."

—Sun Tzu, The Art of War

"They tell us, sir, that we are weak; unable to cope with so formidable an adversary. But when shall we be stronger? Will it be the next week, or the next year? Will it be when we are totally disarmed, and when a British guard shall be stationed in every house? Shall we gather strength by irresolution and inaction? Shall we acquire the means of effectual resistance by lying supinely on our backs and hugging the delusive phantom of hope, until our enemies shall have bound us hand and foot? Sir, we are not weak if we make a proper use of those means which the God of nature hath placed in our power."

—Patrick Henry

If you take nothing else from this book, I hope you at least have a good understanding of what true discernment is and what it means for you. What is discernment? According to the definition given by Merriam-Webster online dictionary, discernment is "the quality of being able to grasp and comprehend what is obscure : skill in discerning" or "an act of perceiving or discerning something."

For the purposes of this book, Discernment is an act of perceiving something that is not readily evident. It is a razor-sharp perception or judgment. It is also the keen faculty that reveals what is usually obscured to others. But, inherent in this definition is also veracity – our capacity to perceive Absolute Truth. It also includes our skill in distinguishing between truth and Truth. Truth with a small "t" is the collection of those things we've come to believe due to our experiences, our perceptions and our buy-ins via various teachings. Truth, with a capital "T" are those things that we Know (capital K for all-knowing) with absolute and unequivocal certainty, due to our direct experiences with God/Prime Creator and irrefutable and Universal Truths that originate from this relationship. Discernment is the first ingredient in Universal Wisdom or the Wisdom of God.

THE IMPORTANCE OF JUDGMENT

As I've mentioned in chapter twelve, judgment is viewed as a negative thing by the "New-Agey", spiritual community. Some will even go the extra mile and quote Ascended Master teachings that speak of not being in judgment. But what many so-called "spiritual leaders" are either not perceiving or not sharing is that there is a clear distinction between *not being judgmental* and *not having judgment*.

We cannot have discernment without good judgment! Being judgmental is an entirely different thing; it is when we hold ourselves out as superior to another and use this platform of "superiority" to criticize and/or put them down. It is often used for the purpose of demeaning, defaming, and hurting.

False-spirituality or misguided spirituality doesn't differentiate between the two. The definition of the two is convoluted to cause confusion, making us less likely to use our judgment. Consequently, we are less discerning. Because we are not discerning to begin with, we don't recognize what is happening. It is similar to a software virus that infects the actual anti-virus software that would normally detect this virus and eradicate it. If the anti-virus is compromised, the virus goes undetected and continues doing damage unchecked.

Judgment equates to sound wisdom. It is your ability to think, to see clearly; to make a distinction between what is right and wrong action and your ability to assess a situation so that the outcome is favorable for all those concerned. Judgment is critical for those that serve the Light of Prime Creator and are embodied to help infuse this Light to everyone on the planet. If we do not use our judgment, we cannot be effective, and so many of us are not effective because we've bought into the notion that having judgment is a negative thing. Here again is a New Age philosophy or misinterpretation of biblical passages and/or other sacred texts and bodies of Higher Teachings. It is one of the reasons the Light Forces on the ground are "losing ground". You can't have discernment without firm, unfaltering judgment, as these go hand-in-hand.

FIRST SIGN IN DISCERNING

How do you become discerning? Primarily, discernment develops with continuous connection to Prime Creator/God. Those things that are in alignment with the Original Blueprint of Prime Creator give off a certain resonance or vibration; and those things that are not in alignment don't have this. It can't get any easier than that to detect what is of Truth and what is not. The challenge is whether we're in "constant" connection with Source/Prime Creator to experience that vibration. If we're not, we will fall for the fakery every time, and we'll always be second-guessing ourselves.

When we're in direct contact with Source, we feel a nudge in our stomach – in our gut. This nudge or disturbance is a warning sign – our first sign of discernment. Here is your "warning center". It is that place that will indicate to you that something isn't right with what is being said, what you're reading, what you're experiencing, etc. Many of us will either 1) discard this feeling or 2) won't even feel it.

When we reject this sensation, we are not giving ourselves credit for being able to tap into Universal or God-Wisdom. We may not think we're worthy of obtaining direct information from Source-Creator, so we discard it and rationalize that we're just stressed or apprehensive about something. If this is the thought process, then we are correct in being apprehensive, as apprehension is our indication that something isn't right and for us to take time to reflect and analyze the situation carefully or quickly get out of the situation. This intuition is a sixth-sense, if you will – one that is tapping into the Realms of Absolute Truth and Light and providing feedback. When we are continuously in direct communication with Creator and obtaining our information and wisdom from there, as opposed to the external world, this type of discernment is spelled with a capital "D" – Discernment. It represents the absolute Truth, Certainty and/or Knowing that can be obtained.

CAUSES OF NON-DISCERNMENT

When we're facing possible danger, and we don't experience the nudge in our stomach, we may not be in-tune with that part of us that is in direct connection with the Divine Realms. It is similar to our radio not being plugged into an energy source. What are some of the causes for not being discerning? This problem is critical to get to the bottom of because it is the reason that many of the Light Forces in a current embodiment are being compromised. Remember, this is a Spiritual War and the other side is not fighting fair. If we're not aware of our weaknesses, the Opponent will find and exploit them – they do this every day. Being non-discerning is probably the biggest weakness we have. It is our Achilles heel! Here are some of the main reasons we're not discerning:

+ Lack of spiritual confidence or feelings of unworthiness

+ Expectation that others (i.e. the Spiritual Industry) will provide correct information and truth

+ Spiritual-Eagerness or Ascension-Eagerness

+ Emotions

+ Clouding of Judgment

+ Disconnection from Source or God

+ Obtaining surrogates or substitutes

+ Attachment to outcome

Lack of spiritual confidence or feelings of unworthiness

We are more prone to put discernment away when we feel unworthy. This unworthiness also pertains to how we perceive ourselves physically, mentally and spiritually. In other words, if we see ourselves as being unattractive, we will value the information and guidance of someone we deem to be more attractive than ourselves. We tend to give credence to those people more because we may feel that being attractive is an accomplishment or that they have an "in" on how to do this. The same holds true with feeling spiritually challenged or not having attained a certain level of spirituality. If we find someone who has a good "talk" and acts the part of having achieved a level of Spiritual Mastery, we will tend to follow the words, advice, concepts and teachings of this person. We justify this to ourselves subconsciously, thinking that they are closer to God or Source than we are, and therefore they must know the Truth. The glorification of another person makes us "star-struck". This behavior is induced by having an adverse perception of ourselves and perceiving another in a more positive manner. Because we perceive them to be "better" than us, we tend to lower our guard and trust them implicitly, in lieu of what our gut tells us.

The Spiritual Industry

Spirituality has become a billion-dollar industry – next in line to the cosmetic and weight loss industries. Unfortunately, it is also reminiscent of the Old West, where every small dusty town had its resident snake-oil salesman peddling his concoctions. If you've delved into the New-Age-Movement-version of spirituality, you've probably come across many who have something that you need for your spiritual edification or, better yet, your Ascension.

Everyone has something to sell you, something you supposedly need in order to take control of your life and attain Spiritual Mastery. But we must be very mindful of what transpires when we're seeking this Mastery or the graduation known as the Ascension. When we're too eager to attain freedom from this dimension/reality and all the hardships that come with it, and someone tells us they have the "magic potion" or procedure that can allow us to jump light years ahead in our spiritual evolution, we tend to put aside our objectivity. Our judgment gets clouded, and we have zero Discernment. When we do not Discern, because we are like excited little kids at an amusement park, screaming with joy when we get on a crazy ride, we are not able to foresee the dangers involved. And some of the repercussions of a bad decision caused by not using Discernment will not become evident until later in the future.

Those in the spiritual industry know that you have a need. The need is to get a grip on your life now or to gain immediate Mastery of yourself so you can get to the graduation party. Like any good salespeople, they will tell you all about their product, services or procedures; then they will stroke your "hot buttons" so that you're kind of salivating at the mouth. They sound so convincing because they have charisma, they seem confident and knowledgeable, and they talk the talk. The next thing you know, you've purchased a new gadget or something else that promises you the ticket to Nirvana. You've probably haven't taken the time to think about possible repercussions. Of course not – this would come with Discernment, and that was not even part of the decision-making process. You were probably too excited and eager to get started with the spiritual concepts, new gadget, psychic healing, reading and/or psychic surgery.

Conditions that lead to Non-Discernment:

1. For some reason, you can't connect directly to God/Prime Creator, although you've tried.

2. You still want to be a part of the graduation: the Rapture or the Ascension. You acquire what I call Ascension-Eagerness.

3. You gravitate to others who claim they have this connection with "Spirit", or "the Universe", or "Mother Earth", or "ETs", etc., and you use them as surrogates for the Creator that you can't seem to get close to. You now put your trust in them and their guidance, teachings, products, services, forecasts and/or procedures.

4. You have *an attachment* to an outcome or eagerness for an end-result. In this case, it's your graduation – Rapture or Ascension.

5. You possess Selective-Discernment. You pick and choose the things that you're willing to sweep under the rug. You look away or "give in" even when good judgment tells you otherwise because the promise of a "positive" result or outcome outweighs your current evaluation of a potential repercussion.

6. Your emotion is the driving force that gets you to act on embracing concepts, obtaining products and/or services that could be very detrimental to you spiritually and/or physically.

7. Your emotion clouds your judgment, and you're not objective.

8. You cease all Discernment because it becomes an obstacle to taking this type of action. You justify taking the wrong action or embracing disinformation by believing that your Discernment skills are not accurate.

9. You put yourself at risk by "buying into" erroneous information and/or purchasing a product, service or procedure that may be detrimental to you in the short-run or the long-run. And, it may have the opposite effect of what you wanted.

Curing Non-Discernment

Direct connection with God/Prime Creator is the cure for non-discernment. There is no other. If you're in continuous contact and communion with Prime Creator and those that serve It in the Higher Realms, your information will be pristine, crystal clear, uncompromised and accurate. If you're in a personal relationship with God-Creator, The All That Is, you will have an excellent working Knowledge of what is and isn't in alignment with Its Divine Plan. When anything is presented to you that is less than that, you will be able to determine that it is a fake or not in your highest good, and it will be easy for you to dismiss.

The idea behind this is similar to detecting a real diamond from a fake one. The real one has intrinsic qualities that the phony one doesn't have. Also, the fake one has certain characteristics that can be observed that give it away as being a fake. For example, if the diamond can magnify the letters of a newspaper, it's a fake. If you can fog its surface with your breath, it's a fake. There are many other detection methods to determine a facsimile. However, it is best when we can ascertain the characteristics and qualities of both the fraudulent and the real one. So, with that in mind, your discernment skills are enhanced when you can identify the deceit and recognize what is Truth – especially what is in alignment with God-Creator.

Also, the next time you encounter an "eager" salesman or saleswomen, observe his demeanor and behavior. Watch this intently and study it, as you may need it later on in life to determine when you're getting bamboozled and sold something you don't want or need – including false spiritual concepts. A disingenuous salesman will display the following behaviors:

1. He finds out what your "hot buttons" are. He will engage you in a lengthy conversation in order to extract from you the information he requires to determine your needs and weaknesses. He's probing to find out what you're emotionally "attached" to or what your desires are. And he plays on this, using this knowledge to manipulate you.

2. He exaggerates the features and benefits of whatever he's selling you. He even creates mental pictures for you so that you can visualize yourself using the product or services. He uses embellished terms, and he fluffs up the information. Sound familiar?

3. He's usually controlled in his delivery. So he's a smooth talker and a charmer. He's also like a chameleon because he can adjust the pace of his speech, tone, and demeanor to match yours. He does this so that you like him and trust him because he knows that many people identify more with those that are similar to themselves.

4. He's good at reading body language and reading between the lines. Therefore, he's figuring you out and formulating strategies of how to sell you and manipulate your decision.

5. He will tell you what you want to hear, even if it's a lie and even if it's not in your best interest. He's there to serve himself, and you are just that opportunity for him.

Why is this of importance? By understanding the mechanics of those things that can hurt you, you can avert them when they confront you. So, if you're not familiar with the techniques of a slick salesperson, who's only looking out for himself, you will find that you've bought "the farm" or a product you can't use, don't need and may be detrimental to you in ways that may not be evident at the moment. Now, if you also study the characteristics and qualities of a *genuine* salesman, one who is honest and helps you reach an intelligent decision, you will probably not fall for the con artists again.

Studying the Opponent's strategies is no different. Therefore, you should learn about how they create the deceit, as this will give you a clear understanding of what these Forces are capable of doing and how they implement their tactics. But more importantly, you *must* Know what is genuine. For example, a well-made counterfeit bill can deceive the general public. The creation of these fake bills is getting more sophisticated every day, and it's a big problem in our society.

Let's say you are a special agent with the FBI and your job is to scrutinize big bills to prevent the counterfeit ones from going into circulation. There are so many astute counterfeiters out there that you can't keep up with their various methods of making fake bills look authentic. You've seen all the different varieties of fraudulent, paper money that have been fabricated up to now. You have used various devices to check authenticity, and as soon as new detection methods come out on the market, a new set of improved counterfeits hit the streets. You can't keep up with the ingenuity of the deceit.

Every other day, you're at some training about a new and improved gadget or technology to be able to detect the latest scam. But the latest and best training you've had up to now is the one that taught you all about the real bills – how they're made, the nuances in each, the special paper, the colored thread, the watermarks, the certain hidden emblems and markings that no one but those who've had this training can detect. You now know all the "ingredients" and components that go into making an *authentic* bill, and you are also familiar with the latest fake ones.

But once you've had this training, all other methods to detect the bogus bills become obsolete. As a matter of fact, it doesn't matter what the latest, improved method is for making these counterfeits. You realize that no one will ever be able to replicate the real thing with one hundred percent accuracy. And since you know what the real thing looks like it's easy for you to spot what isn't. The counterfeiters won't know about the hidden things in the bill that act as safety mechanisms against their replication. It's by knowing what the actual paper money looks like that you can detect the fakes – without any devices. You know because you've experienced the "real deal" so that you can't be fooled!

Isn't this the same when you need to Discern? It's by Knowing what is in alignment with Prime Creator and experiencing Creator and the Higher Realms that you come to Know what is and isn't Truth. How can you Know this if there is no connection with the "Real Deal"/Prime Creator? Connecting to It begins by making the choice to do so. There has to be a burning desire in you to "Get Back to Source" – to the basics, to the fundamentals, to our "True Cradle".

The reason that our lives may not be where we expect them to be, especially when we're practicing spirituality, is that we may have been connecting to everything but Prime Creator. We've been substituting the connection with quick fixes – inferior facsimiles of the "Real Deal". We've been connecting to counterfeits; and because we're not vibrating to our highest potential due to illnesses, poor choices, and our desire to hold onto surrogates and disempowering belief systems, we're being messed with by parasitic, astral entities in service to the Dark Forces. No wonder we're all "marching to the beat of a different drummer" and can't get our stuff together, or get on the same page about anything. Maybe it's time we let go of the baggage that we've collected while traveling off the beaten path. Maybe it's time we travel light, and get back on the straight and narrow road. This road takes us on that journey that reconnects us with God-Source, Prime Creator. It is this connection that will activate your Higher Discernment. There is no other way, and there is no more time to waste.

CHAPTER 15

KEYS FOR SPIRITUAL WARFARE

*"Until one is committed, there is hesitancy,
the chance to draw back, always ineffectiveness."*

*"Concerning all acts of initiative, there is one elementary truth the
ignorance of which kills countless ideas and splendid plans: that the
moment one definitely commits oneself, then Providence moves, too."*

*"All sorts of things occur to help one that would never otherwise have
occurred. A whole stream of events issues from the decision raising in
one's favor all manner of unforeseen incidents and meetings and material
assistance which no man could have dreamed would have come his way."*

—As told to Goethe by W.H. Murray

It is imperative to Know how to play the game in this realm and
who the key players are that's why studying the Opponent is so
important. It is one of the most important components of our victory – the Light's victory – because it gives us insight on how to
maneuver through the Opponent's traps and all the hurdles set up
by them. Remember this is the "game" of war, a spiritual war. It is a
game of strategy – where the prize is our souls and ultimately our
liberation from third-dimensional reality.

It is wise to take this very seriously, as your skill-set in this war game determines how it will turn out – victory for the Dark Forces or victory for the Forces of Light. Based on the amount and severity of heinous events that are manifesting in the outer world at this moment, the scale is tipping in favor of those Forces that are very organized, on the same page about their strategy, their goals and their methods – and it's not The Light. These Dark Forces are disciplined, not divided and not arguing amongst themselves. They have a strategy, and they're focused on achieving their goal. They are skillful, strategic and flawless in their execution.

And to recap: the Light Emissaries – or the ground troops of the Light Forces – on the other hand, are too busy trying to recoup from disintegrating relationships, drama, illness and other unpleasant situations that are thrown at us by these Nefarious Forces to keep us from uniting and fighting back. We would have eradicated the darkness on the planet by now, not just because we're greater in numbers, but because of the potential Light-quotient that we carry. There is also one critical fact that we keep forgetting. We have the Authority and Power of Prime Creator, when we make a conscious decision to tap into that God-Stream or Flow of God.

It is part of the plan of the Dark Forces to keep you spiritually crippled, by tampering with your spiritual self-esteem, with your *Knowing* and your soul memory. This way, you think you need to seek your spiritual strength and obtain your answers from outside yourself. By seeking externally, be it through the internet; teachers; living masters; gurus; Low-Vibration, discarnate guides that reside in the Astral Realm; and pseudo-spiritual leaders, you are stating that you don't trust your spiritual acumen. You are also communicating that you're disconnected from the "Cosmic Ocean" or Creator-Essence and that you prefer to get answers and guidance from other sources, which you consider are more valuable and "connected" than you are and more accurate than God-Source.

If you are obtaining your truth and guidance and DNA upgrades and whatnots from outside sources – meaning everyone but Source/Prime Creator – you can rest assured that the information, advice and/or procedure is more than likely compromised. Why wouldn't it be? If I were the enemy, I would use every avenue at my disposal to jeopardize my opponent. I would infiltrate my enemy's camp and disseminate *disinformation* via the different methods at my disposal – methods that I know will be effective.

With respect to Spiritual Warfare, I'd go with the so-called channelers, pseudo-spiritual teachers and leaders, and those who claim to be "Masters" and gurus – the spiritual imposters. I would feed their egos and stroke their "hot buttons". And because their Discernment capabilities are not fine-tuned, they make perfect candidates for passing along the disinformation. Again, these pseudo-teachers and spiritual leaders have lowered their vibration to such a point that the low-vibratory, Dark Forces can readily access them. These Forces will now communicate the disinformation they want to have disseminated – and these teachers and leaders, otherwise known as hosts, are "happier than a fly on poop" to oblige.

When you go directly to Source, on the other hand, there is no opportunity for hijacking the information. There is no chance of tainting it or misinterpreting it, and it can't be hidden, tampered with or garbled. Direct connection provides for clean, clear, transparent and pristine information that comes from that place where everything is Known; everything is in Balance, and everything is Perfection, according to The Divine Blueprint. It is the Truth, and it stands naked – with no ornamentation or embellishments. There is no need for interpreters, channelers, or other means of delivery. The line of communication is open and is between you and God/Prime Creator. With this open channel of communication that has always been at your disposal, why would you need to go anywhere else for guidance or answers?

The reason this happens is because you don't know who you *really* are. You have identified with being a mother or father, clerk or manager, sinner or victim, rich or poor. You have heard that you are a Divine Spark of Prime Creator. You may understand the basic concept, but you don't actually embrace it – subconsciously, you are uncertain about it. You need to Know this to be true in your heart. It is not a belief, or something you take on faith, as this leaves room for doubt. A Knowing is the fact that it is a *Certainty*. It is an unequivocal Truth, one that cannot be changed and is not prone to interpretation.

Knowing who you are is the most important part of this whole conversation. Without this knowledge, you become the pawn of the Dark Forces. All sorts of disempowering propaganda and disinformation campaigns will be launched at you in order to get you to establish a belief system that keeps you dependent on others for your physical and spiritual wellbeing. It is intended to prevent you from directly connecting to Divine Source.

If you don't know who you are, it will be very difficult to achieve Mastery over this current experience. You will always be chasing the proverbial carrot, and never reaching it because all the skills needed to reach it – we have been told – are developed by taking classes and obtaining information provided by compromised sources. It is a brilliant strategy that the Opponent has. In contrast, these Dark Forces are skilled masters. They're not following different beliefs. They don't have opinions.

As disturbing as this sounds, this Opponent and those working on its behalf are worthy of admiration. They are so on top of their game and so successful at Spiritual Warfare, we should be modeling our warfare tactics on theirs. For example, every time a Light Emissary lacks Discernment and embraces disinformation, the Opponent has won another battle. Even worse, each compromised person spreads the Opponent's deception to others, and they set it up so that we take ourselves out through animosity and in-fighting in the so-called spiritual community. Because we're oblivious to their tactics, this ignorance makes it easier for the Opponent to keep winning. If we observe their skill-sets, we will learn a lot of techniques that will help the Light Forces that are in embodiment now. Everything that they do that we don't counteract makes them stronger and allows them to advance! Let's explore what gives them the edge over us in this realm.

Positive Aspects of the Opponent's Behavior

+ Unified
+ Focused
+ Skilled
+ Diligent
+ Organized
+ Goal-oriented
+ Driven
+ Flawless Execution of Tasks

Things the Light Emissaries need to do to be more efficient:

1) **Unification** – We have a myriad of spiritual philosophies and understandings that keeps us divided. There is only one Truth, and that is found by going within and connecting to God/Prime Creator. Not understanding the "collective mission" will keep us scattered and docile and make us easy prey.

2) **Responsibility** – We have to begin by taking a stand and being engaged in this world and start taking *proactive action*. When we stand down and wait for external forces to make things happen, we allow the Opponent to advance unrestrained.

3) **Reclamation of Power** – We need to have more Discernment with the information that we read and listen to, especially with

respect to those that claim to be channels, guides from the Astral Realm, teachers, and spiritual leaders. Looking externally for our illumination is a means of disempowerment. We reclaim our power by:

+ **Staying in a Place of Neutrality or Equanimity** – When we give in to our negative emotions it leads to bickering amongst ourselves, animosity and discord that serves to lower our vibration and divide us. This process strengthens the Opponent. (This concept is discussed more in *Getting Back to Source: Tools of Connection, Protection & Empowerment*)

+ **Knowing Who We Are** – We need to have the confidence that we are Emissaries of the Light and the spokesmen/spokeswomen for the Light. We are imbued with the Essence of Creator. Not recognizing who we are, in truth, makes us vulnerable to those that are willing to guide us with "untruths". It makes us dependent on them for our spiritual growth and creates weakness in us that the Opponent takes advantage of by exploiting us every chance it gets.

+ **Continuous Communion with Source** – Not connecting directly to Source-Creator on an ongoing basis for communion and infusion of *Its* Essence disempowers us. It allows the Opponent to steer our ship and provides us with corrupt information for our spiritual navigation that stagnates us.

+ **Spiritual Humility** – Spiritual arrogance and self-imposed aggrandizement of spiritual attainment are another Achilles Heel for the Light Emissaries. It plays into our ego, as we inadvertently put down others that are not within our standards. This behavior causes us to lower our vibration by contracting our consciousness, instead of expanding it. Being humble and detached, and in a state of awe – like a little child – allows us to be an empty vessel to be filled with the Essence of God. Thus, we are in direct connection to Source and our consciousness expands, and our vibration is raised. When this happens, we become impervious to the grip of the Dark Forces. It's also the demeanor of a True Spiritual Master.

4) **Awareness** – This entails our desire to be fully aware of what is transpiring in the world and understanding the Forces that co-exist with us, who are busy designing and implementing the conditions that are evident in the physical and Astral Realm. This understanding positions us to make better choices and become more efficient when we take action in correcting what is not in alignment with The Original Blueprint.

5) **Recognition of the Tactics** – Hate, fear and separation are some of the tactics used against the Light Emissaries. We must stay objective and in full Discernment when we hear, see or read things that are clearly meant to create hate and fear of groups or individuals, and cause separation. Not staying objective and experiencing hate for another lowers our vibration and makes us easy prey. Also, do not help to fuel this hate. If we are helping to spread this, we become the carrier of this hate-virus, and we will be responsible for the consequences, as this action is a choice using our free will. Falling into the "hype" or "witch-hunt" or blame/hate movement is a possession by the entities serving the Dark Forces. This behavior is not indicative of Mastery or a representation of a Higher-Vibratory Being serving the Light and Divine Plan of Prime Creator.

6) **Re-Grouping** – This is when we realize that what we've been doing up to now hasn't been working. Then, we need to have the willingness and humility to learn from our mistakes and correct what has gone awry in our spiritual path and with our ability to be "way-showers".

7) **Learning from the Opponent's strategy** – We need to be willing to study the game plan of the Opponent, as a sports team would study the moves of its opponent. Learning from their

successes and our weaknesses will give us the insight we need to make corrections in our strategy and acquire the skill set we need to make substantial progress.

8) **Staying Ahead of the Opponent** – Staying several steps ahead of the Opponent requires excellent observation. When we are aware of how they operate and understand when and why they interfere in our lives, and negatively impact our world, we can then change the outcome. The good news is that the Opponent's strategy or game plan is very predictable and obvious. It follows a particular pattern and formula.

9) **Being Sharp and Awake** – We need to have a clear understanding that some of the Light Emissaries that are currently embodied, who don't know who they are, and/or who haven't stepped into their Divine Power and Authority yet are:

+ Vulnerable
+ Predictable in their behavior and thought processes
+ Experiencing low-vibration emotions, like:

    a. Anger

    b. Arrogance

    c. Disdain

    d. Doubt

    e. Fear

    f. Hate

    g. Sadness/Sorrow

    h. Stubborn Pride

+ Are not effective
+ Are being influenced by disinformation
+ Are easily used to aid the Opponent
+ Create an identity based on their experiences in *pseudo-spiritual movements* or their interactions with this Lower-Vibrational Realm

+ Show a disconnection from Source-Creator

+ Incorporate the beliefs provided to them by compromised outside sources

So direct connection with Prime Creator/Source is the only way you can activate your Knowing of who you truly are. You recognize yourself as being like a thimbleful containing the ingredients found in the Essence of Prime Creator. Once you embrace this Truth, you become instrumental in bringing the changes that are so necessary. You cannot activate by having someone tell you that you contain Divine Essence. It takes Direct Experience with The Divine in order for you to fully understand with your *Knowing* that this is Truth beyond all truth.

You cannot understand this with the mind – it is something that is felt in the heart, in every cell of your body and every atom of your being. It is accepted with humility and gratitude. Then you become infused with the Knowledge, Wisdom, Power, Strength, Courage, and Full Authority of Prime Creator. There is nothing that you cannot do, nothing you cannot Know, nothing you cannot attain, nothing that you cannot correct and nothing that you cannot transcend. Then you are empowered to help restore balance and the unfoldment of the Original Blueprint back to this Lower-Vibrational Realm – and birth a new era.

CHAPTER 16

CHANGING OUR PREDICAMENT

"Awareness of the suffering of others, and finding the compassion within you to help alleviate it, allows you to embrace the ultimate expression of your humanity."

"Alleviating another's pain, helping them to become empowered, witnessing their path to self-realization and mastery are one of the greatest achievements and rewards that one can attain. This trait is found in those whose essence is one with the Divine…"

"The greatest evidence that we lived is to leave behind our imprint in the lives of others by aiding them in reaching their maximum potential."

—**Ari Kopel**

How do we emerge unscathed from the challenges we face? What do we need to do collectively to ensure that humanity can reach its maximum potential, to create a world where everyone has a chance at experiencing peace, joy, honor, respect, dignity and self-realization? How do we change our spiritual perspective from working on only ourselves to helping others achieve transformation? What needs to happen so that we can become empowered to take the right action when it's needed? These are some questions to ponder. But the most important one is what are we willing to do to change our thinking and our beliefs in order to become instrumental in effecting change?

You see, if you are not willing to look inside of yourself, to see what constructs you're holding in place that make you ineffective, you will just be another organism on this planet that consumes. Because you're of higher intelligence, you'll also keep yourself entertained by philosophizing and dreaming of other realities to experience while never being immersed in the present one. And that will just about sum up your existence and experience on Earth.

Uncovering what's holding you back is only the beginning, however, for if you're not willing to take action, you're still helping to keep in place a reality that is not sustainable, functional or equitable for the rest of humanity. How is this so, you ask? Well, everything is a fractal or a smaller replica of a bigger version of itself. What is found in this smaller section is identical to what one finds in the larger one. It is the same concept as the microcosm being an exact duplicate of the macrocosm. Everything that happens in the microcosm is also contained in the macrocosm. So, the layout of an atom is a duplicate of what transpires in the cosmos with planets orbiting around a sun, for example.

When you choose to not actively participate in helping to find solutions or implement change, you may think your choice doesn't have an effect because it's an isolated event. You think that you are not part of the bigger equation – also known as life or Creation. But, in reality, we're all interconnected, and when you think this way, a lot of other people also do. Similarly, your thoughts are a fractal of the collective thoughts of others and of what is transpiring in the world at large. When you feel that your lack of participation in creating change won't matter, those who are trying to effect change don't make much progress. This is because those that get out of their comfort zone and attempt to make a difference face an enormous, energetic barrier or "wall" of resistance called apathy, complacency and indifference – a wall that is a monumental task to overcome, given the relative few that undertake this feat.

There are many who take a back seat to things because the path of least resistance is much easier than the route of action. It takes an exceptional person to get out of their comfort zone and do something that puts the limelight on them or makes them do the type of work they're not used to. Those sort of people are far and few in between, while those who leave it up to others to "take care of business" are a dime a dozen. So this observation should give us an indication of humanity's predicament.

This lack of desire to participate in life in this manner is also a frequency that is emitted by you. It is transmitted into the "collective unconscious", and others who have the same propensity for inaction will pick up on it and are affected by it. It's like their radios are tuned to that frequency. As others emit this same frequency, it gets amplified. And it becomes a signal that broadcasts indifference, apathy, defeat and consent to be enslaved.

As I mentioned throughout this book, there is much evidence that those meant to help instill a positive transformation on this planet have been thwarted by a very cunning and adept opposition. There are too many of us who are not "fully present" in this life; not participating; passing the buck on our "pre-embodiment-commitments". We spend a lot of time and money on finding ways to "bailout" via extensive meditations, ET rescues, opening of portals or a so-called Ascension. Therefore, it is very clear that a great deception has taken place, one that has decommissioned most of us.

What has occurred is too blatant for us to ignore any longer. And yet there are those who choose not to acknowledge how we've all been compromised; how spirituality has been hijacked and used against us. Many of them proclaim to be "enlightened" even while acting as agents of the very forces they profess don't exist. If we don't use our Discernment to detect these forces at work, we will continue to be farmed like cattle.

STAYING ON TASK

What does it mean to "stay on task" with respect to changing our predicament? For the purposes of this book it means being no-nonsense, being focused, and having a definite course of action. Flying by the seat of our pants may not be the right choice or most efficient strategy considering what we are facing as a species.

That said, we may need to adopt different modalities or tactics that will help us create the world we want. If we are building a house, let's say, we have to be very focused on the construction of it. If we aren't, the house will come out lopsided or perhaps have a weak foundation. You need to make sure you have the ideal piece of land, the correct measurements, the right tools and materials, and experienced labor. If you cut corners or slack off, the structure will probably have defects.

Similarly, if you show up to the construction site thinking, "Let's see what my fate brings me today", the house may never get built at all. A laissez-faire attitude creates a lack of momentum to execute the job. It's like being commissioned for a job that only you are skilled at, then spending the workday thinking about the cruise you're taking on the Rhine River next month rather than the task at hand. The quality of the work will more than likely suffer, as you are not present; your body is there, but your mind and heart are elsewhere.

This behavior is found in many who are presently embodied on this plane of existence. The attention is kept on things that take us away from this reality and the present moment. And as a consequence, we mess up on achieving our maximum, life potential. We put a damper on our ability to effect change by dreaming of an "Ascension", the definition of which has been given to us by the Opposition.

EFFECTING CHANGE

While we're here, in this reality, let's make the best of it. We're here for a reason, as pleasant or unpleasant as the experience has turned out to be. Escapism is not responsible behavior or indicative of Mastery. Spending your time and energy and incarnation trying to find a way out or fervently seeking out the next life without having Mastered this one is a cop-out. It's like being in kindergarten and not paying attention to the lessons in penmanship, vocabulary and reading because you're too busy daydreaming about the doctoral dissertation you'll write for your Ph.D. This behavior will obviously jeopardize your ability to get a Ph.D., since you will have missed the skills you need to write the dissertation at some point in the future.

Becoming fully present in this life, in this reality, is essential for integrating our physical with our spiritual selves. When we are aware of the events that are happening around us and in our world, we have an opportunity to respond, to be proactive and change the outcome. We take action in both the physical and spiritual realms. And we don't deny the physical just because we are primarily spiritual beings. We are both at the present moment, as this is the "template" used to correct that which is out of balance in this density. One aspect of ourselves doesn't negate the other, as both are necessary for the task at hand.

The tools needed to engage and navigate in this world are:

Openness – This is a state of mind in which we're like a blank slate, taking every circumstance and situation as a unique experience without qualifying it with preconceived ideas or definitions. It is also a state of "allowance" or "surrender", where you only function as someone infused and unified with The Essence of Prime Creator.

Non-Attachment – You help for the sake of helping. You take "right action" for the purpose of correcting an imbalance. You are immersed in the moment of the action without expecting anything in return. You are detached from any outcome so that the action or "the doing" is "the journey" and the "transformation" at that moment.

Objectivity – This means you observe without qualifying or defining. You examine what is in front of you as a "detached observer". You are in a state of equanimity. From this position, you can then make a correct choice by using your Discernment.

Judgment – You use sound judgment to make sense of what you are observing, experiencing, hearing and thinking. Good judgment allows you to understand the situation in front of you and helps in formulating right action. It gives you a sense of whether to act or not and what level of action is required.

Discernment – You have Discernment (with a capital D) when you tap into the God-Current or God-Essence that is "All Knowing" and Divine Wisdom. Once you're in that space or "inner realm" – as this Essence is within you – you know as Creator Knows, and you can decipher what is Truth and what is not. You will "Know" what is in alignment with The Divine and what is not. Based on this "Knowing", you can navigate through the clutter of information and the plethora of potentially inappropriate choices.

Compassion – When you merge with Prime Creator, you see with God's eyes and feel with God's heart. You then Know and Love all Creation and see everything – Every "thing" – from the perspective of that Creation, living thing or human being. You see yourself in others, and others see themselves in you. True Oneness with The Divine is experienced when you embrace everything in Creation with respect, dignity, honor and reverence. You also exert compassion when you stand up for the right of others to experience joy, safety, balance, peace and freedom to express.

Action – Creation doesn't manifest without action. It originates from a thought or inspiration, but then it requires work in order to birth. An artist receives an inspiration for a painting. He begins to formulate the overall concept in his mind. He decides on a topic or theme and then selects the color scheme. He picks the medium he will use: oils or acrylics, pastels or watercolors. He chooses the brushes or palette knives, the canvas or paper. Then he gets his arm and hand to follow the instructions from the brain – according to the blueprint within his mind – to manifest his creation. If his physical is not engaged in the process, the artwork remains in the mind, unreachable for others to experience.

You may have many potential "masterpieces" within you as well. You may have ideas or designs that will create alternative energy, or you may have poems that will touch the lives of others in a very profound way. Whatever it is that is still within you, which is not yet expressed or birthed, needs to come out. It could be what is needed to alleviate someone's suffering – or make peace with a condition that afflicts them. But if the idea or words of inspiration never take physical form, the blessing is stomped.

We have the capacity to ignite the human spirit and inspire change by taking action and bringing God-Consciousness to this realm. We need to lead by example. We accomplish this by co-creating with the Ultimate Architect and Designer. Each of us is, therefore, the spark that blazes a trail for change. Don't ever believe you can't do something that is inherent in you to express and act on, especially when what you bring to this world exemplifies Godliness and helps others connect with Source and their own God-Potential. If you think you can't or that you've got this or that condition that hinders you, this is a deception! Intrinsically, you are glorious, powerful, wise and an agent of change, love, peace, and balance.

How do we change our predicament? We choose to be fully present, fully aware and take action in whatever capacity we can. The delusion that we can just sit under a tree meditating and visualizing a new world is great, but it falls short. The missing piece of that formula is action, and it has been taken out of the equation by false spirituality. Action could be as complex as organizing a protest or as simple as sharing an article and letting others know about this information. Whatever it is that you feel you can do to advance the efforts of the Light and help alleviate the adverse conditions on the planet is a step in a positive direction.

CHAPTER 17

ASCENSION

"Surrounded by stinging wasps, I watched them beat their wings in slow motion. At that moment, I recognized them as being one with God. And I was left unscathed and transformed..."

—**Ari Kopel**

You may be of the school of thought that we need to aspire to "go somewhere" to a new Earth, perhaps a fourth or fifth dimension. This idea is fueled by New Age information that, again, isn't the complete truth. This concept also comes from the New Testament, when Jesus "ascended" into heaven; however, the notion of going somewhere because we've attained a certain spiritual level or Higher Consciousness could be misinterpreted and misunderstood.

The "Ascension craze" peaked right around the winter solstice of 2012. When nothing transpired, and people didn't magically materialize in a Higher-Frequency Earth or other Realm, there was a tremendous letdown. But that didn't stop anyone from obtaining more information from channeled sources and so-called spiritual experts who pulled answers out of the ethers as to why "the Ascension" didn't happen just yet. The newest update is that it is really meant to happen at a much later date. They may genuinely believe this, or they may have pushed the date forward in order to squeeze a few more dollars from the sales of tickets for workshops and events. The new marketing for this could sound something like: "We're on the cusp of this great 'event', come join us at our portal-opening ceremony!" Unfortunately, not too many will see through this deception; they may not have surpassed their discernment shortcomings or their attachment to the "elusive" Ascension.

Ascension is defined by Merriam-Webster.com as "the act of **rising** or ascending; *especially*: the act of **moving to a higher** or more powerful **position**". Based on this simple definition and observing the negative aspects of humanity, are we moving upwards, emulating Godliness? In other words, is our consciousness expanding, reaching towards God-Consciousness; are our actions more responsible; are we more loving? Is the world a better place, or is what we see in the world an indication that we are devolving or descending into an abyss?

How do the so-called Light Emissaries measure up? Are we connecting with Source-Creator or are we listening to discarnate beings and others? Are we primarily in service-to-others or are we too self-absorbed? Are we using our Discernment and making correct choices or are we embracing beliefs and concepts that are not in alignment with Divine Truth? Are we attempting to Master ourselves or are we spiritually arrogant and putting down others? Are we coming from ego and a separation from Creator, thinking we created this reality or are we coming from a place of humility and gratitude? Are we too busy working on our personal spiritual graduation or are we trying to uplift others so that they too have a chance at this so-called "event"?

If we were to define "Ascension" as an expansion of consciousness that only leads us to eat organics, not drink fluoride, become vegan, meditate for ten hours, practice yoga, attend drumming circles and sweat lodges, we have a very high probability of not experiencing this event in our lifetime. While these activities can be beneficial and show that we think out of the box, real Ascension requires greater inner work and a much higher awareness than that.

This "Higher Awareness" occurs when we connect with the Mind and Heart of Prime Creator, which then allows us to experience God-Awareness. It includes Awareness about all the beautiful and ugly aspects of this world. This Awareness is one that enables us to observe the ugliness and the unspeakable darkness with objectivity and courage. The purpose of this is not to just acquire an acute awareness about everything that negatively affects this world, but to instill in us the backbone to take the action necessary as a response to this awareness. How many of the so-called "enlightened" actually take a stand or have that inner fortitude? There aren't many, for the reasons already discussed in this book.

THE ELUSIVE ASCENSION

So why hasn't the Ascension happened yet? Again, it's because it's not meant to happen – at least not the way you've been told or anticipated. Do you want to hear a fantasy and deceptive information? If you do, I can point you to thousands of sites, blogs, and videos that will lie to you. The Ascension hasn't happened because you haven't yet made the conscious choice to infuse yourself with Prime Creator. You see, the Essence of Prime Creator is within you at all times. You exist and express in this realm or any other realm because of this Spark or Essence.

Allowing this Essence to expand in your being, becoming consciously aware of It at *all* times, and acting from the Consciousness of Prime Creator at *all* times is the "Ascension" you seek. So, in reality, there is nowhere to go. You become one with Creator right here, right now! You are in fact allowing God-Source to express fully through you, similar to completely opening up a faucet and allowing all the water to gush out. When you close the tap just a bit, you will get a trickle. When you close it even more, you'll get a couple of drops. When you close it all the way, you'll get nothing at all. It is the same when we disconnect ourselves from Source – we think we're on our own and do everything on our own. But all along, the "Cosmic-Ocean Current" is in the pipes, ready to flow when you decide to turn the spigot.

The Truth is that you have never been separate from God-Creator – ever! But your choices are everything! Recognizing this Truth is everything! Desiring to reconnect is everything! You don't need to go anywhere to enter that Higher State of Consciousness that is evident in those Higher-Dimensional Realms, as Creator dwells in you and always has. You just allow *Its* Essence to fill you – again, you open up the faucet!

The expansion of your consciousness occurs when you, 1) embrace this Truth and 2) operate from this Higher, God-Consciousness so that you're emulating Creator in your physical form. Then everything falls into place. Your life starts working; your health improves; you grow some backbone and spring into action; you start effecting change in your life, in your community, and in your world. You are protected from negative conditions and situations, and you are shielded from psychic and demonic attacks. Your vibration is raised, and your expanded consciousness and higher frequency have a positive impact on others, as you participate in bringing back the Divine into this realm. How to connect with Creator and recognize Creator is discussed in *Getting Back to Source: Tools for Connection, Protection & Empowerment*, the sequel to this book.

ASCENSION

When I "choose" to connect with Source-Creator, and I do this every moment I can, I tap into a Force that is all encompassing. It is a feeling as if I'm taking a deep breath and then exhaling. It's a feeling of being full and satisfied – and I feel complete and whole. When I feel this way, I "Know" that I am in that Presence that is undeniably the Presence of God-Source. There is a feeling that is familiar and indescribable, as no words in human language describe it. My being recognizes Home, Truth, Joy, Harmony, Balance, Wellness, Abundance, Nurturing, and Total Acceptance via Unconditional Love. And I receive the blessings of Ultimate Wisdom and Truth.

That said, I also have to live on this physical plane, which includes, among other things, earning a living. I often spend time contacting companies I do business with and speaking to the folks in customer service. Some of these folks are members of what is termed "the sleeping masses" - those who are not yet aware of certain "hidden" truths about this world because they're caught up in the everyday minutia of living in the Matrix. They show their disdain for their job and believe they were dealt a bad hand in life. When they answer the phone, for example, they make you feel like your call is a bother, your questions are ridiculous, and your situation is taking up their time. They sound jaded, cynical, bitter, angry and resentful – in short, they have an attitude.

When these individuals address me in a belligerent manner, things get interesting. What I choose to do is not feed their negative attitude, which is exerting a negative frequency. Instead, I counter that by modulating it, replacing it with a much higher one. So, I address them with reverence, honoring who they are. I speak to them in a genuinely loving tone. And this means that I recognize their True and Higher Self, and I speak to that being who is also One with the same God-Source that I am. I tell them that I respect their expertise and their ability to help me. I let them know that I am grateful they are there for me and can answer my questions and concerns. I express to them that they are great at what they do. I make sure to recognize their level of professionalism and desire to help. I speak to them in a humble and grateful manner, with no expectations of an outcome. So, if nothing goes my way, I'm okay with that, and I will still honor them and be grateful for having taken the time to help me.

When I communicate with another human being, who is just another me, with problems like me, who is disenchanted with life, my "Higher Frequency" – emitted by my words and the tone of my voice – acts like a key unlocking their heart, and the real being that is locked up within the confines of disillusion and ego is set free! Then we're communicating heart to heart, soul to soul, and we recognize one another as One. The Divine and God-Potential in that person becomes activated! As I have consciously practiced this, the transformation in people has never failed me yet.

What is the Ascension? It is the act of chiseling away what is surrounding you and giving you an identity – the false beliefs, false spirituality, detrimental ego, sense of separation, opinions, barriers, perception-filters, regrets and all the concepts we've embraced to help us make sense of our life – and liberating the real you. Who is the real you? The real you is the one who never left the heart of God. It is the one that is pristine, crystal clear, uncontaminated, whole, transparent and imbued with all the ingredients of Prime Creator. It is like chiseling away at a piece of solid, petrified coal to get to the magnificent, translucent diamond!

And when you discover this Truth, the Truth of who you really are and choose to connect to that Ocean of Infinite Wisdom, Power, Joy, and Divine Love, you carry this Divine Essence in your essence, in your demeanor, in your thoughts, emotions and actions. And you address others using this Divine Essence so that these Higher Frequencies – that you now personify – can unlock the hearts of others so that they too find the Essence of the Creator within them. When they start using this Higher Frequency, their comportment changes, their thoughts change, and their actions change. And they begin communicating in a more loving manner, seeing life differently, finding a purpose and inspiring transformation.

What is the Ascension? We are! The Ascension is here and now – when we choose to connect to God-Source in this manner and chisel away those aspects of ourselves that are no longer needed. The Ascension is recognizing that "in Truth" we all contain the ingredients of Prime Creator and that when we choose to embrace that and personify that, we help others identify this within themselves as well.

So the key to all of this is to become God-like right here and right now while still living in this reality. Then we will transform this realm back to the Divine, Original Blueprint, and the Higher Realms will be experienced on Earth. We do so by letting go of the baggage and the old constructs that have kept the "coal" in place. Once we chisel away all that is not needed, we liberate the eternal Spark of God within us that can now shine and inspire others to do the same. That, my friend, is the "Ascension". It is as close as your heartbeat, as subtle as a gust of fresh air and as simple as taking in a cold drink of water.

CLOSING THOUGHTS

The Dark Side never sleeps. We are in those times that require us to be in Full Discernment and Full Vigilance. If we're not, we'll wake up one day and there will be nothing left to fight for or wake up for. Many of us have been ingrained with a dislike of the word "fight" or "Warrior". The truth of the matter is that the Opponent will not just hand over this world and our freedom because they are loving and kind – or have had a change of heart. We need to take this world back, and it is a fight that takes place at many different levels, not necessarily in the physical form. What should we be fighting for? We fight to hold on to what is still decent and wholesome in this world, what is innocent and kind, pure and Godly. We are losing these qualities and losing our humanity.

By not being cognizant of what is truly happening behind the scenes, we'll think we've made progress when indeed all we've done is open the gate for the Opponent. By not standing up to this, we're giving our consent to adverse, planetary conditions and the further enslavement of humanity. Those that say, "there is no evil", or "let's not focus on the negative", or "we bring into reality what we focus on" – without understanding that these concepts are too generalized, as are all "Truisms" – are helping to keep in place the suffering that is experienced on a grand scale. There are many that adhere to this philosophy of not focusing or thinking about the negative, yet the occurrences of evil and transgressions against all life are escalating. Is it possible that by not looking at a problem, in order to have the opportunity to find a solution, exacerbates it instead? Wouldn't this be the obvious conclusion of any intelligent, responsible person?

Standing idly by or sticking our heads in the sand is irresponsible behavior and making us active participants of the takeover of humanity. This behavior is evidence that those who hold these ideologies are severely compromised by the Opponent, who wants to convince us that there is no Opponent and that if we dwell on it, it then becomes a reality. The reality is that the Dark Forces are real and well, and more stealth and clever than we are. In our desire to escape this reality, we are taking the spiritual opium they have offered us and have been rendered a non-threat to their plan.

Because of the pernicious times we're in, there is no more acceding to spiritual self-indulgence or the kind of separation we engage in when we insist on defending our ideologies. It is a time to find common ground. This task should not be that difficult when we realize that connecting to God/Prime Creator is the only solution. If we did connect we would quickly Know that the "Highest" Love and Compassion, Understanding and Mercy, Grace and Ease, Strength and Courage, and Truth and Wisdom have always been at our disposal. Anything that is not coming directly from Source-Creator has a very high probability of compromising us so that we are ineffective in this embodiment and don't attain our Spiritual Mastery or our liberation.

If we become instruments of hate and fuel the hate or help to disseminate disempowering propaganda and falsities, and our actions cause harm to others, we will suffer great consequences, as nothing goes unnoticed in this universe. And this is why Discernment is so necessary for our spiritual evolution. Because we have free will, we have the ability to make decisions. Making wrong choices could lead us to participate in things that are supporting the Dark Forces and their agenda, and thus we become accomplices to this most serious of crimes.

We also have the choice to connect directly with Prime Creator and obtain all our guidance, strength, wisdom, courage, opulence and authority from total infusion with God's Life-Stream. And to do so is also a choice. Does it take work? Yes. There is no free ticket to any ride worth taking. Is there effort involved in receiving sweet, bite-sized portions of marshmallow, inserted with the bitter lie-pill, and then gift-wrapped to make you more receptive to it? No. And receiving false spiritual guidance and untruths in this manner is no different.

Uncovering "The Great Mysteries" of God requires a burning desire and great self-discipline. When we decide that this is our path, we go into the Great, Universal Sifter or Universal Funnel. Here is where the most refined and polished "souls" will find safe passage, not because one is better than another, but because of one's resonance or frequency match. The higher the frequency or vibration, the easier it is to pass through the "narrow opening" – the "eye of the needle". And again, that higher vibration is acquired through Self-Mastery and selfless service. Going through "the eye of the needle" is a *rite of passage* for those that have served The Light of Prime Creator without wavering, without questioning, without deviating. Then we can approach the True Holy of Holies. We enter in humility, reverence, and awe, and we enter because we've earned it.

In truth, we are the custodians of this world. Many of us, who know better, are making the conscious decision to not step up and take responsibility for it. Many are not even inspired to help turn things around, or taking an interest in the unprecedented conditions engulfing the planet – conditions of injustices and cruelty.

Yes, many of us heard the call and came to this world by the droves. The problem is we then forgot why we came and who we are. We redefined the reason we embodied and became immersed in the everyday minutia of the incarnation. Those that remember why they were called, and are still engaged in participating, are weary and heavy-hearted. Many have been vigilant and proactive, at such a high level, and for such a long time, that it's not physically, mentally, emotionally or spiritually sustainable any longer. And to add insult to injury, these few are carrying the weight of the burden for the rest of the "sleeping" Light Forces, for the sake of humanity. But their efforts are not making a bit of a difference. Nothing is changing because this is not a job for the "Lone Wolf". It takes all of us – this is why so many were beckoned. Otherwise, only a handful of avatars would have been sent in. It's time for a major reboot and reassessment. This undertaking cannot and should not be done by just a handful – it takes all of us. There is no external event that will magically come and change things. We are that change, and it is a group effort. Even Yeshua Himself didn't go at it alone!

There are two sides of the fence. One side is a world of illusion and delusion. This world, you'll find spiritual charlatans and quacks, snake-oil peddlers and court jesters that will sell you every lie imaginable to keep you within the confines of that fence. Then there is the world on the other side of the fence. On that side, you'll find Truth, Justice, Compassion and Empathy. On that side of the fence, we actively create our world based on the principles of what is Godly and Holy, what is Fair and Just, what is Pure and Balanced. On that side, everyone helps one another earn their place in the Kingdom of Heaven.

What side do you find yourself on? What are you willing to do to gain your true liberation and help others attain theirs? Do you take the path of least resistance and only worry about taking care of yourself, or do you take the narrow road and touch people along the path, bringing them along with you on the journey? Do you live in denial or indifference with what transpires to others across the world – those who don't have a voice, those who are not known? Or are you different? Do you stand up and move mountains, or kneel and plant gardens? Do you shout it or sing it, paint it or write it? Are you just passing through this incarnation, and when you're gone nothing has changed? Or are you here because you are the change? Remember that a Master dwells within you. Remove the layers that block the radiance of the diamond, and there you shall find your True Self!

You are at a crossroads, and it is time for you to make a choice. I hope you choose that road that not only brings you the fulfillment of the inner riches of the real Kingdom of Heaven, but the one that also grants you the joy of bringing these inner riches to others. It may not be the easiest road or the fastest road. It is the path with the fewest footprints – footprints that have been eroded by the sands of time. Those who walked this way helped plant the seeds of True Wisdom, allowing everyone the opportunity to partake of the fruits of Higher Knowledge. Their footprints may be faint on the road now, but the essence of their passage through this realm is there nonetheless.

I hope that once you embark on this road, it leads you to a life of eternal blessings and that you finally experience the "Return Home". I hope you discover that "Home" has always been within your heart. And on that day, my friend, may you experience boundless rejoicing, accompanied by all those whose lives you've touched, loved and blessed along the way.

GLOSSARY

Archons – According to the Nag Hammadi texts, which are the intact records of the Gnostics found in clay jars buried in Nag Hammadi, Egypt, the Archons invaded Earth about 3,600 BC and were like a virus. These off-world beings had the ability to duplicate reality or distort it in order to fool us. They do so by getting into people's consciousness, manipulating their reality and making them act the way they wouldn't normally. They're also responsible for the deterioration of culture, especially when the culture is trying to emulate what is in alignment with The Divine. The Gnostics described these beings as looking like a reptile and others like fetuses (similar to a gray alien). The definition of Archon is a high official, lord or ruler.

Ascended Masters – Those Illumined Beings who serve Prime Creator in helping to restore the Will of God/Creator back to Earth. These Beings have achieved Self-Mastery and have obtained their liberation from the life-death cycle and this plane of existence. Their vibratory rate is very high, and they are not readily seen with our physical eyes. Those that are real Ascended Masters are recognized via their unique energy signature. They are meek, humble, in service to humanity and ready to provide assistance when asked. They respect free will. They will work with you only when asked. They do not seek to be worshiped, and they do not communicate via a channeler. See *Channeler/Channeling*

Astral Realms – It is that realm right above the physical/ third-dimensional realm in frequency/ vibration. It is comprised of a lower version and higher version. The vibrations found in the Astral Realm are not as dense as in the physical one; therefore, there is no density. You'll find thought forms, emotions and entities that are of low-frequency residing there. Most psychic attacks, paranormal activity, channeled messages, discarnate beings, and those that serve the Dark Forces, such as demons, djinn and poltergeist, for example, originate from this lower version of the Astral Realm. Most "expressions" that reside in this lower version are highly sophisticated in their knowledge yet have not reached a very advanced level of spiritual evolution. Most deception and disinformation comes from those entities residing in this realm – regardless if they are of the higher or lower version.

At-One-ment – This definition gives a more proactive meaning to the original Atonement. Atonement has been defined as reconciliation with God, especially in the pardoning of Original or general sin, by the death and resurrection of Jesus the Christ. At-One-ment is when we become One with Prime Creator by merging our consciousness with Its Consciousness, our will with Its Will. We then partake of Its Love, Grace, Nurturing, Perfection, Wisdom, and Power.

Beings of Light – These are Beings whose primary function is to serve Prime Creator. They are representatives of the Positive Polarity and Highest, Light Emanation of Creator. One of the duties of these Super-Luminal Beings is to make sure the Will of God/Prime Creator is implemented and restored. They reside in the Higher-Vibrational Realms, closest to the Bosom of Creator. Some even serve in the capacity of Lords of Light, Elohim, Elders, Archangels and Ultraterrestrials. See Ultraterrestrials

Bosom of God – The Bosom of Creator is the True Holy of Holies or the "inner sanctum" of God. Here is where *Every* "thing" comes to rest and infuses itself back with the whole Essence of Prime Creator. It is that place where everything is in balance, vibrating to the frequency of Creator. It is Creator at Zero-Point – where it experiences Itself as Its Creation, returning to Itself.

Channeler – A channeler is a person who has the ability to act as a conduit or venue for information given – usually in real time – by an entity, discarnate being or off-world being (of extraterrestrial origin) or other so-called councils and groups originating in the Lower Astral Realm. The entity or off-world being usually takes over the body of the channeler, in order to deliver the message/information. Often a voice or speech pattern, including accents that don't belong to the host/channeler, can be heard as the message is being given. Other things that can be detected are strange mannerisms and/or behaviors that are not typically displayed by the host.

Christ Consciousness – It is that state of being where we are acting, thinking and feeling as a Christed Being. A Christed Being acts, thinks and feels from a state of equanimity; is in reverence to All life; is in a humble service to All life, and is imbued with the Divine and Essence of Prime Creator. A Christed Being's very existence is to be infused with the qualities of God/Creator and to emulate It, becoming the vessel that manifests God's Plan in any of Its Creations. He/she displays God-compassion, God-mercy, God-love, God-forgiveness, God-nurturing, God-humility, God-reverence, God-kindness, God-empathy and God-understanding. He/she respects and honors all of God's Creations. Christ Consciousness, according to Paramahansa Yogananda, is "The projected consciousness of God immanent in all [Creation]."

Contemplation – Contemplation means to fix one's attention upon God/Creator and/or the different aspects of Prime Creator. Contemplation is an active action, as opposed to the passive action of meditation. With contemplation, we have the desire to make a connection with God/Creator and to infuse ourselves, consciously, with Its Totality; thus, we experience as Creator experiences. This deliberate action allows us to view any situation from God's perspective; thus we obtain the Highest Truth and the most pristine understanding.

Cosmic Umbilical Cord – This umbilical cord is our direct line or connection to Prime Creator. It is that line that we need to keep consciously open and unobstructed so that God-Essence and God-Wisdom can freely flow into our being. It can also be called the Silver Cord or "life-thread" that anchors The Spirit of God into our physical bodies and also serves as the "lifeline" that keeps us attached to Prime Creator. Many see this cord during Astral Travel.

Dark Forces – The Dark Forces are in direct opposition to Prime Creator. Those that are in service to the Dark Forces harbor the lowest, vibrational frequency and usually dwell in the astral or low-vibratory realms. The Dark Forces or Opponent include, but are not limited to: Archons; the Cabal, which are those on this planet that control the world or shadow government; Dark Lords; Demons; Djinn; lower-dimensional and negative ETs; Fallen Angels; Lucifer; Poltergeists; a negative ET race known as Reptilians; and Satan. These are considered the minions of the Dark Forces. Their mission is not to uphold the directives or the protocols of the Divine Blueprint of Prime Creator, but to destroy it and place themselves as rulers over this realm and humanity.

Demiurge – The term refers to those gods that were created by Prime Creator to create other worlds and seed these with life. These are also those beings that were responsible for genetic manipulation of the higher intelligence of a world and who were worshiped as gods, as a consequence. A demiurge is a being or group of beings that take on the role of a creator. Some come from Higher -Vibratory worlds, and others come from other dense, physical worlds in space vehicles. These are not The All That Is, or Prime Creator, as this Supreme Force, and Intelligence is shapeless, genderless, beginningless, endless and nameless.

Djinn (Jinn) – Also known as genies, Djinn are supernatural creatures that have been written about in the Quran. They are said to come from the Astral Realm or a universe called Djinnestan, another universe beyond this one. They can take on human form and can be good or evil. Some are tricksters and also possess people. They can be conjured up using magical rites in order to perform services. They are often confused with demons, but they are not the same. The Djinn have the ability to propagate, and they are shape shifters.

Divine Blueprint – The Divine Blueprint is the Original Blueprint, Plan, Design and Intention of Prime Creator for all Its Creations.

Divine Spark – Can also be equated to the spark that could have occurred during the Big Bang, but here it means the life-giving ingredients or God-particles that is found within all Creation. It is also the breath of Prime Creator that breathes life into Its Creations. It is Its Essence and Life-Force that is infused in all of Its Creations. It allows them to express, develop, ascend and descend in consciousness, and hopefully desire to merge themselves with the Whole Creator.

Download – See Transmission

Duality – Duality is something that is experienced in lower worlds. In some of the lowest Realms that are created, as Prime Creator lowers Its vibratory rate in order to compress Its Light, duality is put into play as a way to create balance. Each portion of this duality is also known as a polarity. Outside of the Bosom of Creator or Zero-point, each polarity stands on its own, yet needs the opposite polarity to balance itself. When there is no balance caused by the Negative Polarity being more prominent than the Positive, we experience chaos. In these lower realms, we experience density, time, space, energy, and matter – things that are experienced in physicality. In the physical realm, for example, opposites like good and bad; black and white; positive and negative; Ying and Yang are experienced. Duality is also our sense of being separate from God/Prime Creator and each other. When we're in ego, we separate ourselves from the Totality of Creator and believe we act alone; therefore we believe it's about the "I" and "self", about "me versus you", and we disconnect ourselves from the Whole, believing that duality is Truth and real when it's really an experience in the lower realms.

Earth Embodiment – Earth Embodiment is the choice to experience this planet in human form. Some of us come from realms that are highly advanced technologically and/or spiritually. Taking on the density of a body on this plane of existence requires that many of us lose the memory of where we came from. Earth is a dense world, part of a low-vibratory realm that is governed by time, space, density, matter and all the physics that govern this reality. Those that decide to be born into a realm as this one, do so because of their desire to have a human experience and for their ability to make choices that will catapult them to their next level of spiritual attainment.

Earth-U, Earth University – Earth is like an institution of higher learning. It provides us with the opportunity to learn lessons based on negative and positive experiences. These are the result of imposed situations and conditions that help us make choices. The choices ultimately lead to our spiritual growth and in turn get us closer to returning to The Bosom of God.

Energy Signature – An energy signature is similar in concept to an energetic fingerprint. This signature is unique to Beings of Light, who are in service to Prime Creator. Their subtle energy fields have a particular frequency or resonance that distinguishes them from another Being of Light. This energy field cannot be duplicated or falsified by the Sinister, Dark Forces. Individuals who can recognize the energy signatures of True Beings of Light will not be fooled by those pretending to be representatives of the Light.

Enslavement – Enslavement is a dependence on a system or government for your wellbeing, for your existence, while on this planet.

The system has been created on purpose in order to hold you captive. It is also the subtle and not so subtle control of how you think, what you think, how you express, how you perceive, what you believe, what you feel and how you behave. You think you have control, but in reality you are being manipulated and coerced to behave in certain ways via marketing, political propaganda and disinformation campaigns. This behavior keeps you in a perpetual "hamster wheel" thinking you are working towards a goal that will eventually provide you with financial freedom and all the benefits that come with that. This elusive goal will not materialize unless you continue to run on the hamster wheel. If you decide to get off, you will fail and suffer the consequences. Enslavement is part of the protocols of an invisible prison known as The Matrix, and it has been set in place by those that govern this lower realm. (Also see Matrix)

ET Commanders – ET Commanders are those who command extraterrestrial fleets or ships. Some of these commanders have communicated with humanity or select individuals via channelers. Those that communicate in this manner have provided information that has been Truisms and some information has been completely inaccurate. True extraterrestrial Commanders or beings tend to communicate telepathically and do not need a channeler. Some of these so-called Commanders are known representatives and/ or leaders of fleets and disinformation specialists tend to use these names when they give deceptive messages.

Fifth-Dimensional Earth – The Earth is presently in the third dimension. According to many in the New Age Movement, the Earth will be graduating to the fifth dimension, with a transitional stop at the fourth. Some in this Movement say we're already in the fourth dimension. The Fifth-Dimensional Earth is said to be Earth in its Ascended State. It is also known as the New Earth. Many are also of the belief that they too will ascend along with Earth to this fifth dimension.

God-Particle – See Divine Spark

God-Realization – God Realization is attained when we completely envelop ourselves into The Divine and infuse ourselves with the Essence of Prime Creator so that we are now one. In this state, we think, feel and act as God/Creator. This is the prize of a mature soul. We reach this state when we have refined our thoughts, emotions and deeds so that we can attain this Oneness with Creator and all Its Creations.

Great Cycle – According to the Maya, the Great Cycle equals approximately 5,125.36 years. They stipulated that a Great Cycle was equal to one "World Age" or one growth cycle. Each growth cycle represented the end of an era of humanity's spiritual growth and the beginning of the next stage in spiritual attainment. Five of these Great Cycles equals one "Grand Cycle" of approximately 26,000 years. A Great Cycle is the period in which Earth transits through all of the 12 signs of the zodiac, taking about 2152 years per sign. An "age" is the journey or time that it takes Earth to travel from sign to sign. Each of these astrological ages represents one month of the grand, Cosmic Year. Civilizations like the Sumerians, Tibetans, Egyptians, Cherokees, Hopi, and Mayans also make reference to this Great Cycle and incorporated it into their calendars.

HAARP – High Frequency Active Auroral Research Program or HAARP is a research program jointly funded by the U.S. Air Force, the U.S. Navy, the University of Alaska, and the Defense Advanced Research Projects that does testing on the ionosphere. According to http://www.haarp.alaska.edu/haarp/gen.html , "HAARP is a scientific endeavor aimed at studying the properties and behavior of the ionosphere, with particular emphasis on being able to understand and use it to enhance communications and surveillance systems for both civilian and defense purposes." According to http://www.wanttoknow.info, "The ionosphere is the delicate upper layer of our atmosphere which ranges from about 30 miles (50 km) to

600 miles (1,000 km) above the Earth's surface." Some HAARP researchers are concerned that disturbing the layers of the ionosphere in this manner will be used for weather control, intensifying hurricanes and even to set off earthquakes.

High Councils of Light – These are the Councils in the Higher-Vibratory Realms that are in service to Prime Creator and work with Its Divine Plan. Those that form part of these Councils oversee the different Creations and put in place protocols that follow the Divine Blueprint of Creator. These protocols are the Divine guidelines set in place that bring the Will of God/Creator back to any given world. These Councils also serve to ensure the Return of intelligent life-streams back to Creator.

Higher Teachings - Higher Teachings is the body of spiritual knowledge and understandings that also incorporate the Laws and Protocols of The Higher-Vibratory Realms of Prime Creator, also known as The Kingdom of God.

High-Vibrational Beings – The Beings that reside in the Higher-Vibratory Realms, closest to the Bosom of Creator, are known as High-Vibrational Beings, Higher Intelligence, The Host of Light, The Heavenly Host or The Host of Heaven. Some of these Higher-Vibratory Beings are Ultraterrestrials, True Archangels, Lords of Light, True Elders and True Elohim. The word "True" is to differentiate between those that are impostors, creations of the Dark Forces. These Higher-Vibrational Beings are in service to Prime Creator. They help administer the Divine Plan and restore the Divine Will of Creator and The Original Blueprint to those areas of Creation experiencing imbalance; and oversee the spiritual evolution of worlds.

Host of Heaven – See High-Vibrational Beings

Illumined Realms – These are the Realms that represent the Positive Polarity of Prime Creator. These are worlds of the highest frequencies, since these are closest to the Bosom of Creator. Other names for these worlds or realms are the Light, the Higher Heavens and the Kingdom of God. The Illumined Worlds are examples of true Peace, Harmony, Bliss, Unity, Balance, Pure Wisdom and Love.

In the Know – This term refers to those who are aware of what is transpiring in the world and are awake to higher spiritual principles. They are truth seekers, and the knowledge gathered is used to connect the dots that help formulate a clearer picture of the world we live and the unprecedented conditions that face humanity.

Interconnected – In this world, everything is interconnected. What affects one thing affects other things. For example, if the bees are dying, then crops do not get pollinated; if crops do not get pollinated, then we have a shortage of food. Another example is if alligators are hunted, there will be an overabundance of birds and wildlife in the Everglades that will throw off the ecosystem. With the two examples above, a group of organisms depends on the other to thrive and/or to keep the balance.

Karma – The saying, "what goes around, comes around" is what most know as Karma. The concept is that the universe seeks balance and will correct what needs correcting to bring such balance. If someone commits an act that negatively impacts another, the perpetrator will more than likely experience a correction in this lifetime, or other lifetimes, that will bring balance to their soul's journey. Sometimes this balance is needed for that soul's spiritual evolution and sometimes it is to restore balance due to a rip or schism created in the universe because their negative act.

Knowing – A "Knowing" is information that you are certain to be true. It is absolute and unequivocal. It is knowledge that you possess that there is no question is true, and sometimes you don't understand how you Know it or how you obtained it. You Know this information because it seems to be part of your being and is crystal clear and in focus. This information is Truth, it stands on its own and there is no repudiating it.

Lesser Light – The Light of Prime Creator becomes compressed to create different, vibratory realms. The further the realm is from the Bosom of God or Zero-point, the lower the vibration, and we experience the least amount of The Light of Prime Creator. Those experiencing Light in these lower realms experience the Lesser Light or the compressed Light of Prime Creator. According to Kabbalistic Mystics, the Light of Prime Creator is obscured due to different veils, experienced in these lower realms. This term also describes those that claim to serve The Light but who are impostors who serve the Dark Forces.

Life-Stream – Another term for the *essence* or *expression* of a life-form is Life-Stream. It is that filament emanating from the heart of Prime Creator that is still attached to It via the "Cosmic Umbilical Cord (see Cosmic Umbilical Cord). It is also an emanation of Prime Creator that infuses itself and expresses as any given life-form to experience Itself through that being.

Light Warrior – Light Warrior means a being or individual whose function is to return The Light back to a realm or world that has been compromised by the Dark Forces. The title describes those that are involved in the Spiritual War and serve The Light and Will of God/Creator. This term is used also to describe those that are on Earth to help restore balance by being fully aware of what transpires in the world and who are in full participation. Their primary goal and function is to return this world back in alignment with The Original, Divine Blueprint of Prime Creator. Light Warriors inspire, are leaders and help create change. They are mostly fearless, meeting negative situations and dark energies head on. Many times, they are "movers and shakers" and lead by example.

Loosh – Loosh is the energy produced by negative emotional discharge by a person who is not objective or in equanimity. It is considered food for discarnate beings, entities, demons and other low-vibratory beings residing in lower realms and in service to the Dark Forces.

223

Matrix – Used for the purpose of this book, the term Matrix represents an energetic prison or hologram created by sophisticated off-world/alien technology and software program. It could also be the creation of intelligent beings or entities that serve the Dark Forces. This energetic field or hologram acts like a fence or cage that surrounds the planet and creates a barrier or a situation like a quarantine that doesn't permit humanity to escape, especially spiritually. It could also explain the purpose of reincarnation as a mechanism for recycling souls to incarnate and maintain the population on Earth as energetic livestock. It is also the term used to describe the condition of living on this planet. That condition is where everything is staged to make it seem as if we're free to do as we wish; when in reality life here is similar to a movie set - staged. This scenario is brilliantly depicted in the movie "The Truman Show", with Jim Carey. He thinks his life is real, but he's in a reality show – more like a social experiment to see how he reacts to the stimuli presented by the "overlords" or producers of the show.

Meditation – This spiritual tool is used to allow us to still ourselves and connect to our inner self, permitting us to find the Creator within us. Part of the meditation technique is to quiet our minds. We do this by focusing on a single thought like love, unity, a ball of light or the point between our eyes on our forehead. That point on our forehead and in the back of our eyes is also the location for our pineal gland, the so-called seat of our soul. Stilling ourselves and going into that silence within permits us to shut down the noise of the external world and connect us with our inner awareness, our Higher Self and the Creator that dwells within us. Once we can master this, and recognize those subtle and higher realms, and pick up on the higher frequency of Creator, we can also readily tap into our Knowing or Absolute Certainty and Truth.

Meekness – This is the quality that those who have Self-Mastery possess. The word connotes a total lack of self-pride and lack of self-concern. It also denotes humility for one's own predicament, and puts the focus on being of service to others. The word also means a mildness of disposition, gentleness of spirit, meekness or a strength of spirit, a disciplined calmness. It is a contrast to anger, arrogance and self-absorption. It defines a person who is not only exerting calmness, but is demonstrating a compassionate service to others.

Miscreation – For the purpose of this book, this term refers to all that which is in direct opposition to the Original and Divine Blueprint of Prime Creator. It usually describes those creations in lower vibratory realms that have been designed and implemented by the Opponent or the Dark Forces to impose its creation and replace the Divine one. This term applies to conditions, situations and biologically altered life-forms and astral entities.

New Age Movement - The New Age Movement is a spiritual mishmash of different religions, philosophies and pearls of wisdom. It draws material from various sources. Some of these include: the Ancient Mystery Schools; the Theosophical Society; Rosicrucian; Kabbalistic Mysticism; Zen Buddhism; Neopaganism; Gnosticism; Astrology; Metaphysics; Christianity; Hinduism and Yoga, to name a few. Many of the ideas and concepts fit into a "one size fits all" set of beliefs that are used to make sense of ourselves, our world and our place within it. Many of the "one-liners" of the teachings are Truisms mixed in with disempowering untruths that are then embellished to make them more palatable and accepted.

New Earth – See Fifth-Dimension Earth

Off World Council – See Higher Councils of Light

Opponent – See Dark Forces

Original Blueprint – See Divine Blueprint

Polarity – For the purposes of this book, polarity is two opposing aspects of God/Creator. One is positive and the other negative. It is similar to what we know as the North Pole and the South Pole or a battery having a negative charge and a positive charge. The Positive Polarity of Creator is The Light, and it is of the Highest-Vibratory level. The Negative Polarity is the opposite. Darkness or a lack of Light is of the Lowest-Vibratory level and depicts some of the characteristics of Negative Polarity. Each Polarity is necessary for the other one to have a purpose and serve the Plan of God/Creator. Both need to be present in order for there to be a perfect balance. When one of these dominates the other in the lower realms or realities, we will observe spurts of chaos or enlightenment that tend to bring back balance.

Positive Feedback Loop – A positive feedback loop is a closed system that sustains itself. The Dark Forces implement a positive feedback loop system. Positive, in this case, is not a good thing; instead, it indicates a favorable gain or gain in magnitude for that which instigates the action or behaviors. For example, let's say a plant emits a particular odor when it is compromised and under stress. There are certain insects that are attracted to this odor and they land on the plant and begin to eat it. Because the plant is now further compromised, it lets out more of this odor, which in turn attracts more insects. These begin to feed, and the plant produces more indications of stress. So, the plant's stress creates more of what attracts the insects, which in turn produces more stress.

Realms – We can understand a realm as being the regions, domains, sectors, provinces, territories or zones designed and established by Prime Creator. Each one has their purpose and vibratory rate. These realms range from positive to negative and are created to balance out Creation in any given universe of Prime Creator.

Reptilians – There is a species of extraterrestrial beings known as the Reptilians. They are named this way because they look like reptiles in their facial features, texture of skin and color. They are shape-shifters and seem to be of a fourth-dimensional nature. They seem to reside more in the Astral Realm. Therefore, they tend to be of lower vibration. There are accounts of these throughout human history and some are said to reside within the Earth in caves and tunnels. They are known to be predators, controllers and enslavers of the human race. These are one of the races of extraterrestrials known as Negative ETs, who serve the Dark Forces.

Return Home – See Bosom of God

Rite of Passage – After mastering a level of spiritual learning, one has entry into a higher level, which includes all the responsibilities at that higher level and all the "spiritual gifts" that also come with it. The entry into the new level can be signified by ritual or ceremony that initiates someone into a higher stage of learning or mastery. These include activations and upgrades to the physical form and the soul of the recipient acquired through their own merit. It represents admittance into a higher level through attainment and mastery.

Samadhi – Samadhi is considered to be by yogis the highest state of consciousness attainable. According to Swami Sivananda, "When the mind is completely absorbed in one object of meditation, it is termed Samadhi. The mind identifies itself with the object of meditation." The meditator and meditation are one. The "I" vanishes and merges itself with the object of the meditation. When this happens the meditator taps into and merges with Creator and becomes a vessel to carry out Its Divine Plan.

Selective Discernment – Selective Discernment occurs when we pick and choose what we want to discern. We become attached to an outcome or are eager to get some result or information. Therefore, we set aside our gut feeling about something, hoping that the nudging was just fear, an upset stomach, stress or anxiety. We overlook common sense and good judgment in favor of the gratification of getting what we want.

Sleeping Masses – These are the members of humanity who are not yet aware of certain "hidden" truths about this world because they're caught up in the everyday minutia of living and surviving in the Matrix. See Matrix

Spiritual Bully – Spiritual Bullies are pseudo-spiritual people who claim to have attained spiritual mastery, yet display arrogance, self-absorption, service-to-self and aggrandizement traits. These people tend to quote Truisms and New Age terminology and phrases as a way to show mastery of spiritual concepts, and this is a tactic used to demean another's perspective, beliefs, and spiritual attainment. The bullying is normally done in a public forum in order to embarrass and quiet the person they're attacking.

Spiritual Carrot – The Dark Forces use deceptive promises to keep us chasing after a spiritual graduation or mastery goals that are not attainable based on false spiritual concepts and teachings. These false teachings are designed and set in place by Dark Forces and distributed via outlets like the New Age Movement and spiritual teachers and leaders of that movement. They provide the idea of a graduation or something that will allow us to escape from this current reality into another one that is far better. They label this graduation Ascension, Rapture or simply waking up to a New Fifth-Dimensional Earth or being whisked away by extraterrestrial beings. The concept of leaving this denser and difficult reality behind for something better is like a dangling carrot, keeping us focused on "the prize" as opposed to the negative conditions that are transpiring in our world.

Spiritual High – Getting high on drugs is one form of escapism. Being "spiritually high" is another, and it's the sensation of being elsewhere and not fully present or engaged in this embodiment. Those who show signs of being afflicted by this are similar to someone under the influence of cannabis or DMT (a psychedelic tryptamine). Those who are "spiritually high" are not totally grounded, and they have skewed perceptions of reality, as they view the world through very filtered and distorted lenses. There is no desire to participate in the world, as the spiritual reality and utopia they're creating for themselves, in their mind, is far more pleasant and blissful. See Spiritual Opium

Spiritual Lobotomy – The concept of a "spiritual lobotomy" is similar to a physical one in that the person experiences a disconnect or severing. A "spiritual lobotomy" disconnects a person from their current reality by engaging in delusional, spiritual practices. These practices keep them out of touch with the world they live in and also keep them out of touch with their health, finances, and other circumstances. The images in their mind are of a perfect world they've fabricated. Because of their disconnection from reality, they can only see the images of the world they've created for themselves and are unwilling to acknowledge any other reality or break out of this delusion.

Spiritual Opium – Spiritual ceremony, group meditations, Truisms, embellished concepts and feel-good words are all triggers that act like opiates. They get a person into that state where they're "spiritually high" and in a spiritually-induced stupor. It causes them to create another reality for themselves where they are perpetually feeling good by practicing spiritual ritual, listening to "sugary" messages and being influenced by others who are doing the same. The practice creates a "numbing" of the individual by eliciting feel-good experiences that need to be attained continuously and topped each time – like an addiction. By being "numb" to external circumstances, this takes away their responsibilities in this world. They become disengaged and non-participants of the real and current reality, keeping them disempowered, apathetic, complacent and indifferent. It also causes an addiction to this state where they're constantly trying to escape their current reality and not take care of what afflicts them or the world at large. See Spiritual High

Third-Dimensional Density – The Third Dimension is the reality or realm we're currently in, where we experience height, depth and width. It is also a dimension of density and where we experience time, space and matter. Most beings in physical form exist in this dimension.

Third Eye – The third eye is an esoteric or metaphysical term for a "mystical" and invisible eye located in the center of our forehead, between both physical eyes. Its purpose is to provide inner awareness and sightless perception through our connection with The Divine Essence of Prime Creator. Our Pineal Gland is said to be the seat where this refined perception manifests; but our connection to Prime Creator is essential to be able to discern what we perceive.

Transmission – Transmissions are one of the methods of communication used by Higher Intelligence, otherwise known as High-Vibrational Beings in service to Prime Creator. This type of communication is unilateral and occurs as a download or "dumping" of information all at once. The individual experiencing a transmission will not immediately understand the message or nature of it. They will not begin to put into language the information given at that moment. Sometimes the information unfolds, with time, as a Knowing and reveals itself in an "as- need-to-know-basis". The information also reveals itself as a feeling. The messages or communication comes in as pictograms or packets of complete information represented as symbols or pictures. Eventually, the individual will put the linguistics in place to be able to express the message given. Another method of communication with High-Vibrational Beings is telepathy.

Truism – A truism is information that is known to be a truth and accepted as fact. These are used by the Dark Forces and their minions to sneak in disinformation and lies. The Dark Forces use these truths because they resonate with most of us, and therefore we take them in without any need for discernment. Along with them, we also accept the lie, thinking it's part of the true information.

Truth Movement – The Truth Movement birthed as a response to all the failed promises and hype fed to people by the New Age Movement. Many were weary of waiting for events that never happened. They were disappointed by the lies provided by channeled information and pseudo-spiritual leaders and upset at finding themselves in the same conditions, or worse conditions, that they were before they embarked into New Age concepts and beliefs. Those in the Truth Movement aimed at getting to the truth about the deceit. Another one of their goals was figuring out who or what was controlling the world. Some of their targets were those called Illuminati, Cabal, Zionism and an extraterrestrial race known as Reptilians. The main goal of the Truth Movement was to expose those perpetrators that were responsible for creating and keeping us within the Matrix. See Matrix and New Age Movement

Ultraterrestrials – The Higher-Vibrational Beings that are specifically watching or overseeing the spiritual transformation and evolution, and consciousness shifting on certain worlds are Ultraterrestrials. These Beings of Light are usually from Higher-Vibratory Worlds, and they use vehicles of Light or Light Ships to travel. They are extraterrestrials because they do not originate from Earth, but because they are in Light Bodies or Higher-Vibration, they are known as Ultraterrestrials, where Ultra means "beyond". Ultraterrestrial, then, means beyond terrestrial and beyond "extra" terrestrial. Their ships are not physical or metallic and are piloted using intention and higher consciousness. They are currently overseeing the Spiritual Evolution program for Planet Earth.

Universal Code of Conduct – The Universal Code of Conduct is the protocol used by the High Councils of the different Realms of Positive and Negative Polarity so that there is agreement on how to engage with the Creations of Prime Creator. This Code of Conduct also addresses what is and is not permitted with respect to interference in any particular Creation and how to reach resolutions to possible varying methods of overseeing and implementing evolutionary programs.

Veil – The Veil is the cover or "spiritual blindfold" placed on those taking embodiment, especially when that individual's soul comes from a Higher-Vibratory Realm or world. Its effect is similar to amnesia, where the person forgets where they come from originally. The amnesia is there so that they don't suffer from the "homesickness" created by the memory of the original world. The individual can then become functional and fully immersed in their new expression and their new world.

Zero Point – See Bosom of God

INDEX

C

F

G

H

M

N

S

U

V

W

X

Y

Z

About The Author

Ari Kopel is a graduate of the University of Miami with a major in psychology and minor in communications. While at the University of Miami, she worked as an assistant to Dr. Cesare Emiliani in the Harold C. Urey Laboratory for Paleotemperature Research, on projects involving the study of Pole Shifts and Ice Ages. She later attended Columbia University, New York, for her graduate studies and worked as the assistant to Dr. Robert Jastrow, director of the NASA Goddard Institute for Space Studies, New York, while also serving as Jastrow's teaching assistant at Dartmouth College, NH.

Starting at the age of fifteen, Ari has had frequent visitations to the Higher-Vibratory Realms to attend meetings and conclaves with the Higher Councils of Light, overseeing the spiritual evolution of humanity. She has also had continuous contact with Ultraterrestrials since the age of seventeen and at that age, she became a Field Investigator Trainee for MUFON (Mutual UFO Network).

Ari is the author of the new book *Getting Back to Source: Tools for Connection, Protection & Empowerment*; the founder of 2012Emergence.com; ShatteringTheMatrix.com and the radio show host and creator of "Shattering the Matrix" on BlogTalkRadio.com.

For her latest books, seminars, and speaking engagements go to: www.AriKopel.com.

GETTING BACK TO SOURCE
Tools for Connection, Protection & Empowerment

Available Online and in Bookstores...

37356751R00144

Made in the USA
San Bernardino, CA
16 August 2016